SUBJECTIVE VISION

THE LUCINDA W. BUNNEN COLLECTION OF PHOTOGRAPHS

SUBJECTIVE VISION

The Lucinda W. Bunnen Collection of Photographs

Published by the High Museum of Art, Atlanta, Georgia

Edited by Kelly Morris.
Designed by Walton Harris.
Color Transparencies by Michael McKelvey
Printed by National Graphics, Decatur, Georgia.

Library of Congress Catalogue No. 83-81149
ISBN 0-939802-17-1

Front Cover: *The Bat: 1940* by Clarence John Laughlin

Acknowledgments

The definition, direction, acquisition, and ultimate display of a coherent collection of works of art entails a multitude of complex tasks. The current exhibition and this catalogue are only the most visible endpoints of an undertaking demanding the commitment of many individuals, each with different responsibilities. In Lucinda Bunnen, the museum is fortunate to have a patron who understands the value of collective effort. The consideration of a group of Laughlin prints to form the basis of the collection stemmed from a suggestion by Vaughan Kilpatrick. Gudmund Vigtel, the director of the High Museum, has steadfastly supported this project. Jay Crouse and Chris Brannock of the Atlanta Gallery of Photography greatly facilitated the seeking and securing of works, and Chris Brannock assisted in assembling biographical information for the catalogue. The percipient judgment of Virginia Warren Smith, whose own art forms part of the collection, has been a continual source of strength.

We are grateful to A. D. Coleman for consenting to write the introduction. Walton Harris designed the catalogue and Kelly Morris edited it. Details of exhibition organization and collection management have been coordinated by Rhetta Kilpatrick, who was ably assisted by Liz Lane and Elaine Taylor. The registrar, Marjorie Harvey, and members of her staff, Frances R. Francis and Carol Graham, responded to unusual demands with their usual aplomb. The exhibition was installed with high efficiency by Jon Speck, Nancy Roberts, and Steve Woods. The greatest debt is to Lucinda Bunnen herself for her generosity, her knowledge, and her vision.

Peter Morrin
Curator of 20th Century Art

Preface

The High Museum's serious involvement with photography began in the summer of 1974 in the wake of an overwhelming response to an A. D. Coleman lecture, co-sponsored by Nexus, the Atlanta photographers' consortium. The strength of photographic talent in our own area, public enthusiasm, and outright demand for a photography program made it clear that this museum would miss out in community art interest in a serious way if we didn't respond.

As luck would have it, an anonymous donor had made unrestricted purchase funds available, and the photography collection was launched. In the last decade, significant purchases have been made possible by the Phoenix Society of Atlanta, the Atlanta Foundation, and Mrs. Everett McDonnell. Arnold Crane of Chicago donated a major group of vintage prints by Walker Evans, and the Life Insurance Company of Georgia gave us twelve 19th century mammoth plates of western scenes. But the vast majority of photographs have been acquired with general funds. The Bunnen Collection signals a new phase of the High Museum's efforts.

As with all beginning collections, our first responsibility was to achieve breadth in this remarkably varied medium, and as a result the museum's collection ranges from the early days of daguerreotypes to contemporary works. In less than ten years, the collection has grown to almost 1500 works. Portions of the collection have been circulated to other museums on a nationwide tour, and many works have been lent to major retrospectives of individual artists.

In the brief history of the High Museum's photography collection, however, it has never been possible to specialize, and so it is with particular gratitude that I welcomed Lucinda Bunnen's offer of generosity. The collection documented in this catalogue concentrates in a way that the museum in its own right has not done, and the Bunnen collection was in part conceived as a way of giving the museum strength in one defined area.

In Lucinda Bunnen, the museum is blessed with a donor who is herself a very talented photogapher whose work has been widely exhibited and collected. She is, moreover, a discriminating collector of photography and a member of the museum's Board of Directors. She is, in short, particularly well qualified to respond to our needs. Above all, I wish to pay tribute to this collection's sense of adventure. As a contemporary expression in itself, it matches the finest qualities of the Atlanta community at large.

Gudmund Vigtel
Director

Foreword

In the Spring of 1981, I approached Gudmund Vigtel, director of the High Museum, with the idea of putting together a group of photographs that would expand the existing collection in a special way. After some discussion we agreed on a collaborative approach. A committee was formed consisting of Peter Morrin (the museum's Curator of 20th Century Art), Jay Crouse (owner of Atlanta Gallery of Photography), Chris Brannock (then director of Atlanta Gallery of Photography), photographer Virginia Warren Smith, and myself. Our function was to evaluate and select works which would then be submitted to the museum's Acquisition Committee for final approval.

Since the High Museum's existing collection was heavily weighted towards traditional approaches to photography, we decided to favor contemporary works that have more subjective and psychological concerns. We agreed on a thematic approach, with our theme being "new ways of seeing." Our intent was to seek images that in some way have extended the parameters of photography—either by providing new solutions to traditional problems or new insights into contemporary subject matters.

Our first purchase was twenty-six Clarence John Laughlin prints. Laughlin is a Southern photographer whose singular vision has been internationally recognized and whose recently published treatise on the "Third World of Photography" served as a point of reference for the collecting that followed. Laughlin's theory posits a third use of photography, beyond documentation and purism. In this Third World, the process of making a photograph is dominated by the human imagination, not the mechanical properties of the camera. Laughlin's goal is to so alter the reality of the object in front of his lens that it becomes servile to his mind's vision. His images are centered in the "needs of the human mind and heart" rather than in an objective portrayal of the physical world around him.

With Laughlin as our point of departure, we began to assemble the collection. The group met every few weeks for two years, during which time we looked at a vast amount of material. Fortunately we were able to consider and reconsider much of the work as the framework of the collection evolved. Differences in taste and preference among the group members resulted in many intense and heated discussions of proposed pieces. However, as the collection began to grow and take its own direction, we found ourselves becoming more of one mind. Certain themes began to emerge, such as the self-portrait and regional consciousness. These concerns, coupled with Laughlin's theory of the Third World of Photography, formed the ideological structure of the collection.

I was particularly interested in supporting living photographers in their new work, rather than acquiring their signature images. And, in addition to many well-known photographers, there are also "unknowns" represented whose work we felt fit our criteria.

I feel that the group of photographs we have assembled offers a provocative look at this stage in photography's evolution. I hope that the growth and excitement we experienced through association with this material will be transmitted to those who view the collection, and further hope that this endeavor will serve as encouragement to other institutions to seek out and support living artists.

Lucinda Bunnen

Introduction by A. D. Coleman

What was widely heralded as the "photo boom" of the 1970s will eventually be seen as a watershed in photography's development as a public form of creative activity.

For a time, it seemed impossible to open the most unlikely publications—*Time,* say, or the *Wall Street Journal*—without learning of some new "record" for the field: a record number of galleries and museums displaying photography; a record number of published monographs on photographers; a record number of magazines and newspapers specializing in or incorporating photography criticism; record auction prices for daguerreotypes, for nineteenth-century prints, for major twentieth-century work—even for that less than *rara avis,* Ansel Adams's *Moonrise,* known to exist in at least 900 copies.

The impact of all this frenzied activity on the collecting of photography was tremendous. New institutional collections were initiated, and existing ones expanded, at a rate which precluded system or forethought. Afflicted by the same variant of tulip fever, private collectors bought according to the latest fads, the day-to-day inventories of dealers, or their own idiosyncracies. Somehow the pertinent Biblical injunction—*with all thy getting, get understanding*—never came to mind.

The reason I've sketched this brief account of recent trends is to indicate the context in which the next phase of photography collecting and curatorship will be manifested. For I believe—and developments such as the Lucinda Bunnen Collection bear me out—that we are witnessing the birth of a new phase of photography collecting, the emergence of a new generation of collectors.

This phase, and those who will shape it, will be by necessity more sophisticated than those who preceded them. The well-conceived and well-tended photography collection has become as elaborate and demanding an undertaking as its equivalent in any other medium. This must lead the intelligent curator or collector to place forethought above impulse, if for no other reason than that sheer whimsicality is no longer affordable.

We don't yet have a full-fledged tradition of collecting in photography as we do in the other visual arts—the medium is still too new, the formal collecting of it a comparatively recent phenomenon. So it's not surprising that most photography collectors, even those whose holdings are quite extensive, have based their acquisitions more on their own likes and dislikes than on any system or theory of unification. Nor is it startling that this also holds true for a great many institutional collections.

But the collection based strictly on chance or individual sensibility is of limited value. Its limits are the limitations of eclecticism itself. Even if provocatively idiosyncratic, such a collection tends to lead the audience away from thought, directing it instead towards taste. Its arguments, if any, are destined to be minor. We'll likely find little insight or true revisionism there—no attempts to uncover important "new" historical figures, or to restore the reputations of maligned and/or discarded ones, or to present us with an overview of the medium's history which in any meaningful way goes against the grain of our received version of that history, or to place contemporary work in cogent juxtapositions which shed new light, thus helping to illuminate the current field of ideas within the medium.

To build a more coherent collection, one with a thematic structure and a potential usefulness, something more than mere taste is required. We are now talking about purposeful collecting, which necessitates definition of purpose on the collector's part. Such a purpose can also be based on the personal interests of the collector, but here those interests are used as conceptual tools, to shape the collection and give it resonance.

The Lucinda Bunnen Collection is a prime—and, in several ways, unique—example of the potential inherent in this approach. Part of its distinction resides in the fact that it was conceived from the outset as an educational tool, devised in active relation to the existing collection of a specific public institution by a group of private citizens—several of them, not coincidentally, practicing photographers, including the donor herself. The methodology by which the imagery was selected and the collection organized—an ongoing, two-year argument among five strongly opinionated people—is no less remarkable. Ms. Bunnen has written about that unusual process in her own statement, elsewhere in this catalogue; I will leave its description to her.

From a critical standpoint, what I find most provocative is the central theme of the collection—and, of course, the imagery itself.

The choice of Clarence John Laughlin as the Bunnen Collection's core artist strikes me as particularly apt, for reasons both practical and symbolic. Laughlin, who is still working in New Orleans, is a living artist; the collection's emphasis is on the work being done in our own time. He is a Southern photographer whose work addresses the history and mythology of that territory; the collection was designed for a Southern museum with a regional constituency and mandate. He is a polymathic artist whose enormous oeuvre has many aspects and avenues; the collection embraces a diversity of styles, techniques, and attitudes. He is a seminal artist, highly influential but under-recognized; the collection stresses process and inquiry over virtuosity and acclaim. And, though his imagery is emotionally grounded in the subconscious, Laughlin is a thinking photographer whose writing on what he calls "the third world of photography" provides the crucial theoretical linchpin for the collection.[1]

Briefly summarized, Laughlin's position is that beyond those photographic approaches we commonly term *documentary* and *purist* there is another, which may take several forms but which treats literal subject matter as raw material and the image as metaphor. If the purpose of the documentarian is *transcriptive*, and that of the purist *descriptive*, then Laughlin's could be called *transformative*: subjective, poetic, romantic, symbolistic, concerned less with seeing than with vision, less with information than with intuition.

For at least the past half-century, this approach has been in disfavor with the photography establishment, whose tastes have leaned toward drier, more formal and/or analytic modes, encouraging the severe restriction of the photographer's technical options. As a result, the work of Laughlin and others who have explored the more openly psychological or emotional approaches and investigated the full range of inherently photographic techniques remains less well known, the tendency they represent less fully examined and discussed in the literature. Despite this neglect, however, that tendency (which is central to photography) endures; those inclined towards it have persevered. That, certainly, is part of the point of this collection.

Given the freewheeling creative atmosphere of current photographic practice, that portion of the audience which has only lately come to photography may have a hard time imagining the outrage and scorn which the pioneering work of such photographers as Laughlin evoked as recently as thirty years ago. Rather than recapitulate that here, I will simply say that such devices, techniques and strategies as the theatrical frame, multiple exposure, image-text integrations, negative printing, and many more which younger artists now take for granted were controversial in earlier times. Those who, like Laughlin, persisted in investigating them paid a price—though they are finally witnessing the vindication of their courageous mappings of those terrains.

The Laughlin imagery in the Bunnen group, twenty-six prints in all, comprises more than a third of the Bunnen Collection at this stage of its evolution. In conjunction with the Laughlin prints already in the High Museum's possession, it gives the museum an appropriately sizeable representation of one of the major figures in the history of photography in the South. Diverse in style and subject, the Bunnen Collection's Laughlins indicate the richness of his total body of work while also offering antecedents for many of the more contemporary images.

Thus the staged events of such very different photographers as Cindy Sherman, Arthur Tress, Richard Hill, and William Wegman can be seen as connected to Laughlin's consistent address to the directorial mode in those *tableaux vivants* he created in the crumbling mansions and cemeteries of the South. Laughlin's concern with image-text relationships helped to open that door through which Rita DeWitt, Leah Karp, Robert Stewart, and Duane Michals have stepped—the latter two, intriguingly, in works whose concerns are quintessentially photographic though they contain no photographs *per se*. The embrace of all the technical means at the photographer's disposal—Laughlin's rejection of the hamstringing attitudes of purism—is variously echoed and expanded upon by DeWitt, Michals, Virginia Warren Smith, Lucas Samaras, Ken Josephson, and Evon Streetman in their use of collage, mixed media, pigment manipulation, and hand-applied image components. Laughlin's alertness to the transient vagaries of light and substance is not unrelated to such quite dissimilar works as those of Lisette Model, Ralph Eugene Meatyard, Mario Giacomelli, Ray Metzker, and Jerry Gordon. Finally, Laughlin's involvement with the South—not so much a naive regionalism as a profound and conscious sense of place—is matched in different ways by Martin Stupich, Emmet Gowin, and William Eggleston.

The thrust of the Bunnen Collection, and the purpose of my preceding comments, is not to suggest direct, self-conscious links in either direction between Laughlin and the other photographers represented, but rather to trace an attitudinal kinship which connects Laughlin's work (including not only his imagery but his stance and his theory) with that which came after. From one perspective, the collection can be seen as presenting the more current work radiating outward from the hub of an earlier, prophetic attitude toward the medium. Looked at in another light, we have a survey of an expansive contemporary attitude revealed retrospectively in its relation to one of its vital progenitors.

There are many connections which can be drawn between the images in this group, more than space allows. Though the Laughlin material is germane in one way or another to virtually all the newer work, there are differences no less noteworthy than the similarities. For instance, there is in the Bunnen Collection a recurrence of the theme of self-portraiture: Judy Dater, Duane Michals, Chuck Close, Lucas Samaras, Elizabeth Turk, W. Eugene Smith (a little-known but nonetheless characteristically brooding image), Cindy Sherman and Robert Stewart are all represented by works which demand consideration within that mode. Though Laughlin has made self-portraits, they have not been a central theme of his; none are in the Bunnen group. The introspection characteristic of much of his imagery may be only another form of the self-scrutiny which manifests itself in the act of self-portraiture. Yet the use of the self-portrait as a vehicle for extended exploration is a decidedly recent phenomenon. The images by Michals, Samaras, Dater, and Sherman are drawn from larger bodies of self-portraiture; those by Turk and Close are composites, single works made up of more than one image.

That commitment to extended form—composites, suites, sequences, and other variants—is also a particularly contemporary involvement. We can find aspects of it in the work of Laughlin (who has long organized his imagery in thematic and/or conceptual clusters), Gene Smith (who stretched the boundaries of the photojournalistic essay to the breaking point), and other earlier workers. But such serial explorations as Samaras's hundreds of self-portraits; Leah Karp's threnody for the victims of mass murder, the "Atlanta Children Notebook"; William Wegman's marvelously goofy games with his late dog, Man Ray; Jerry Gordon's water/swimmer suite; Josef Koudelka's dreamlike gypsy chronicles; Ray Metzker's rigorously intellectualized "Pictus Interruptus" sequence; and Emmet Gowin's ongoing family album, now well into its second decade as a public narrative—structures such as these, though not uncommon today, are very new to photography. The size of the Bunnen collection makes it impossible to do more than hint at the scope of the larger works from which these images have been extracted, yet its annotation of this development is important.

Another revealing aspect of the collection—so obvious as to be easily overlooked—is the presence of so much color photography, and the implicit assumption that color is no less viable a photographic form than monochrome. The work included here is quite varied: in addition to examples of some of the accessible color-printing technologies by Jerry Gordon, Laurel Simmons, William Eggleston, and Joel Sternfeld, there are works produced with the Polaroid instant-print systems (Samaras's SX-70; Wegman's and William Larson's 20x24s; and Close's triptych, produced with the 40x70 camera, literally a *camera obscura*—a dark room with a lens in its wall). Moreover, there is imagery involving what is often called applied or synthetic color: the oil-painted Duane Michals self-portrait, the gum print by Stephen Livick, the hand-colored pieces by Evon Streetman, Rita DeWitt, and Virginia Warren Smith. During the period when Laughlin was creating the bulk of his work, none of these would have been acceptable *materials* for "serious" photography. Today's photographer may question
1 their appropriateness for his/her work, but their validity as creative options is unquestionable.

Though the Bunnen Collection in its present form stands as a self-contained entity, it resides within the larger collection of the High Museum. Its presence there cannot help but result in interaction with other material in the museum's holdings. The museum's existing collection was built over the past decade under the direction of Gudmund Vigtel. Though its emphasis is on the classic and traditional, it includes a range of material whose richness is automatically amplified by the arrival of the Bunnen Collection. In addition to the already-mentioned Laughlin material, the museum also holds work by Eggleston, Wegman (a video piece), Laura Gilpin, Richard Hill, and several others in the Bunnen group. Beyond those evident connections, there is other work already there—by such artists as Diane Arbus, Scott Hyde, Andre Kertesz, Anne Brigman, Manuel Alvarez Bravo, John McWilliams, Paul Kwilecki, to name only a few—which bears directly on the issues raised by the Bunnen material. Thus the potential for the Bunnen Collection's future as an aspect of the High Museum's service to the scholarly community and the general public includes not only the possible expansion of the Bunnen Collection as such but its function as a probe with which to examine and refine the institution's larger relationship to photography.

To conclude, then, let me reiterate my conviction that the major public and private collections of the future will be those which approach the medium systematically rather than eclectically. They may scrutinize a specific theme, genre or mode; they may survey the work of an era, or group, or region; they may focus on a working method, or even a particular material. But I believe that an increasingly sophisticated audience will begin searching out and paying respect to those collections whose coherent structures organize the medium's imagery in diverse and meaningful ways.

The Lucinda Bunnen Collection is, I think, an important experiment along those lines. It will be instructive for all of us to observe its growth and its impact on the development of the High Museum's collection as a whole—as well as on the regional audience's perceptions of the medium during this next decade. The field of photography collecting is still new enough that there are no hard and fast rules. At the same time, precisely because it is a relatively uncharted area, the dedicated collector in photography is in a position to make a valuable contribution to our understanding of the medium, by helping us to see more clearly where it has come from and where it may be going.

Note

[1]Clarence John Laughlin, "An Introduction to the Third World of Photography," in *Edward Weston and Clarence John Laughlin* (New Orleans: New Orleans Museum of Art, 1982).

SUBJECTIVE VISION

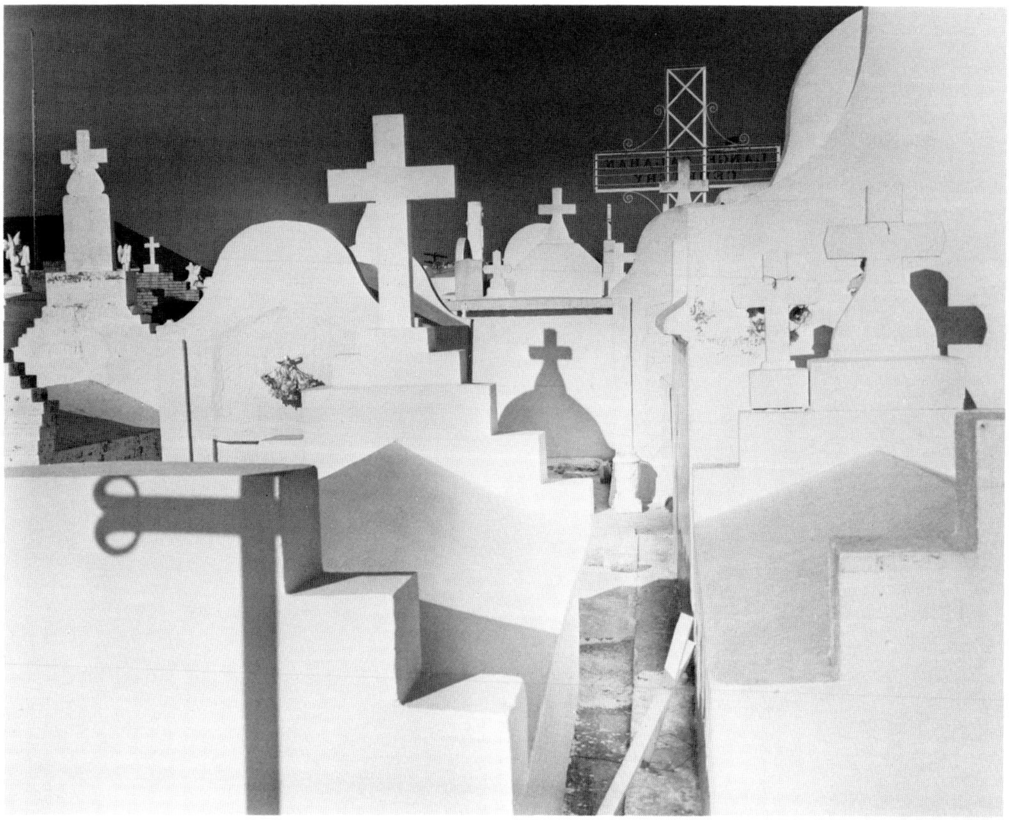

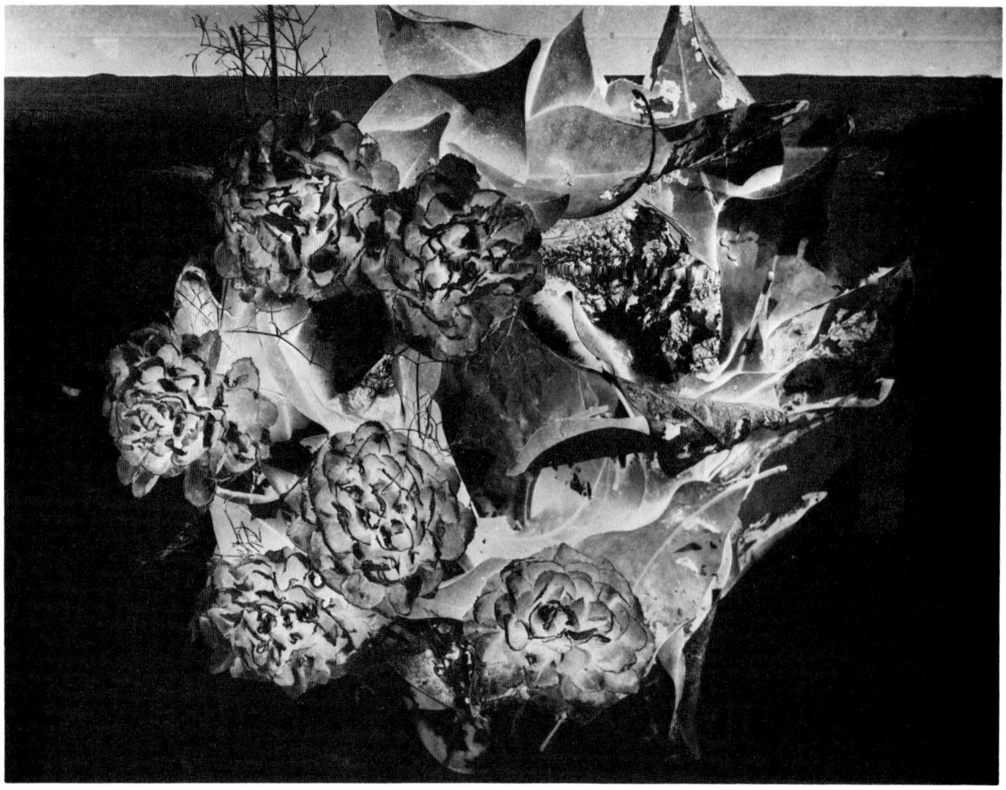

Clarence John Laughlin, *Solidity of Shadows: 1953*

Clarence John Laughlin, *Flowers of the Night Land: 1958*

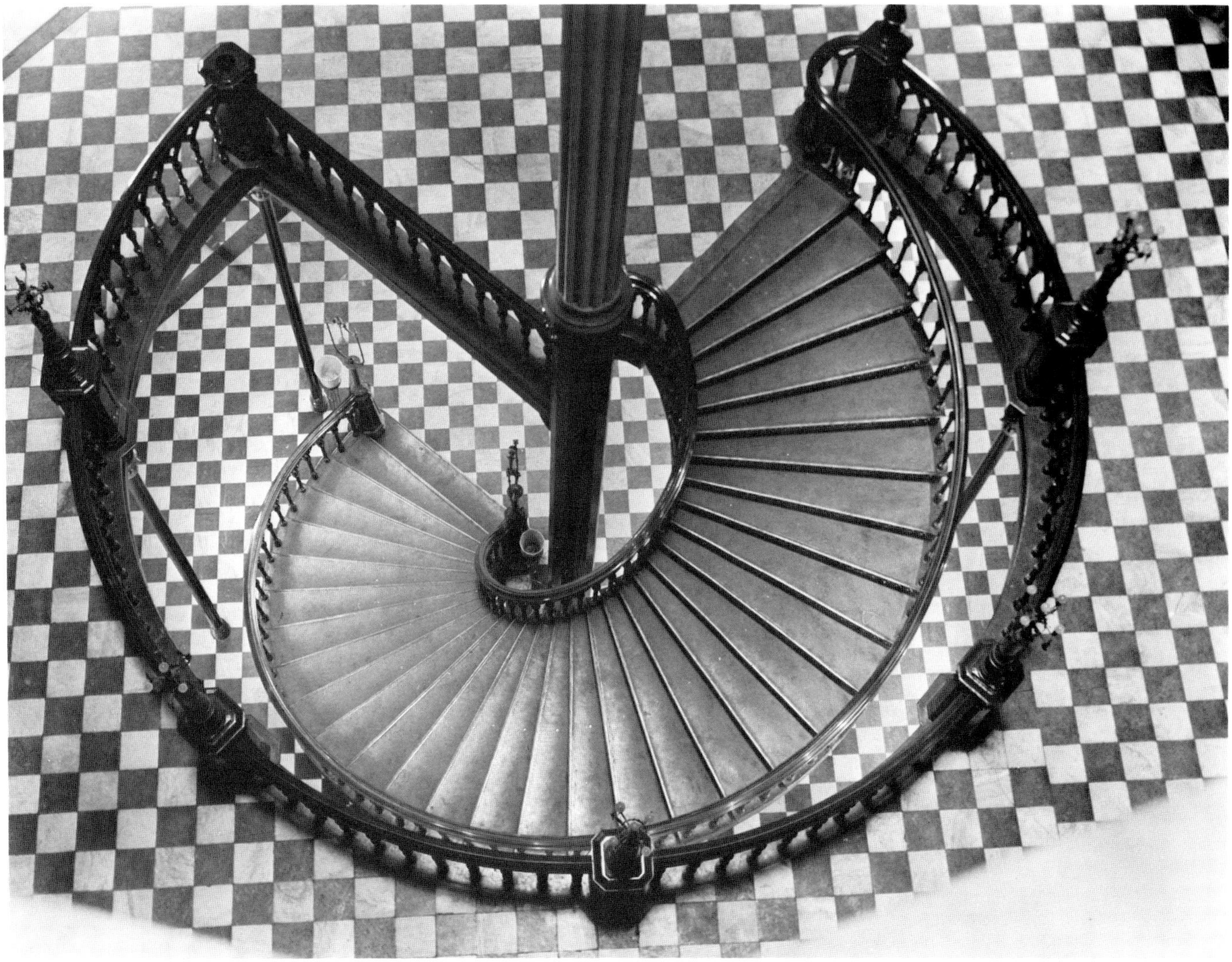

Clarence John Laughlin, *The Iron Shell: 1949*

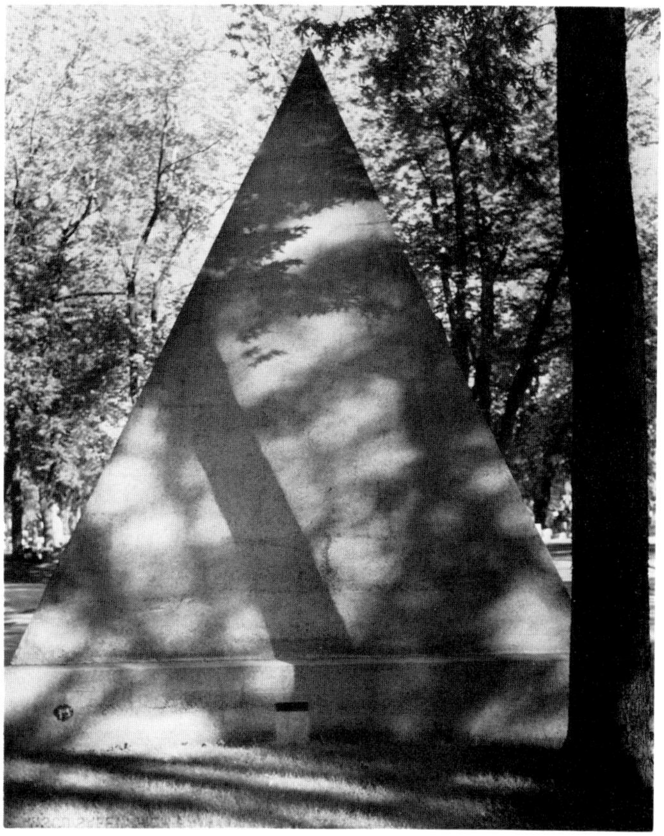

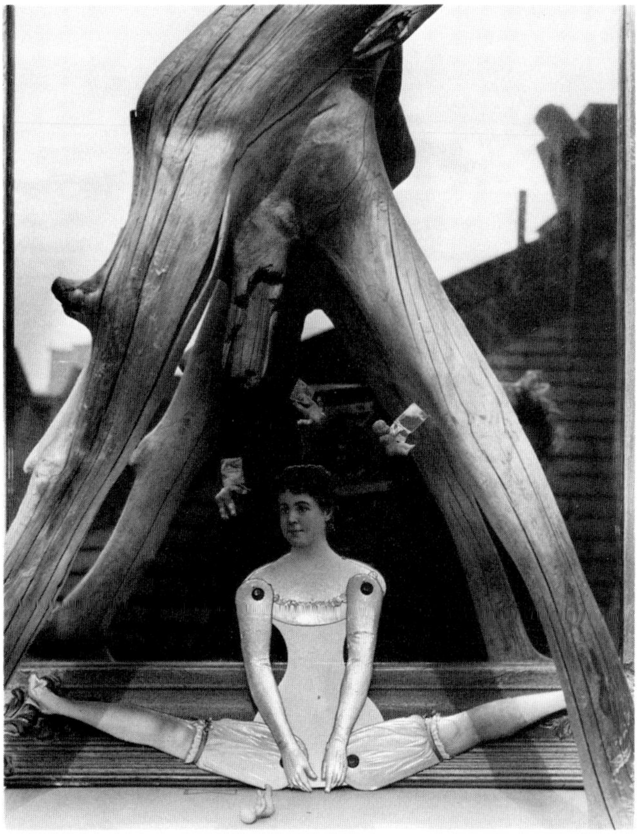

Clarence John Laughlin, *The Translucent Triangle: 1964*

 Clarence John Laughlin, *"Haveth Childers Everywhere": 1952*

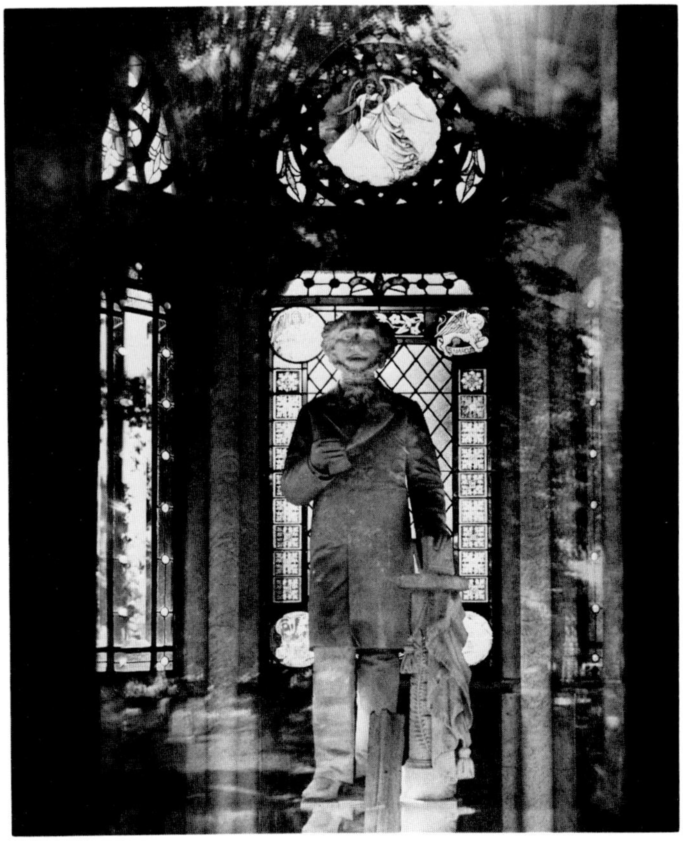

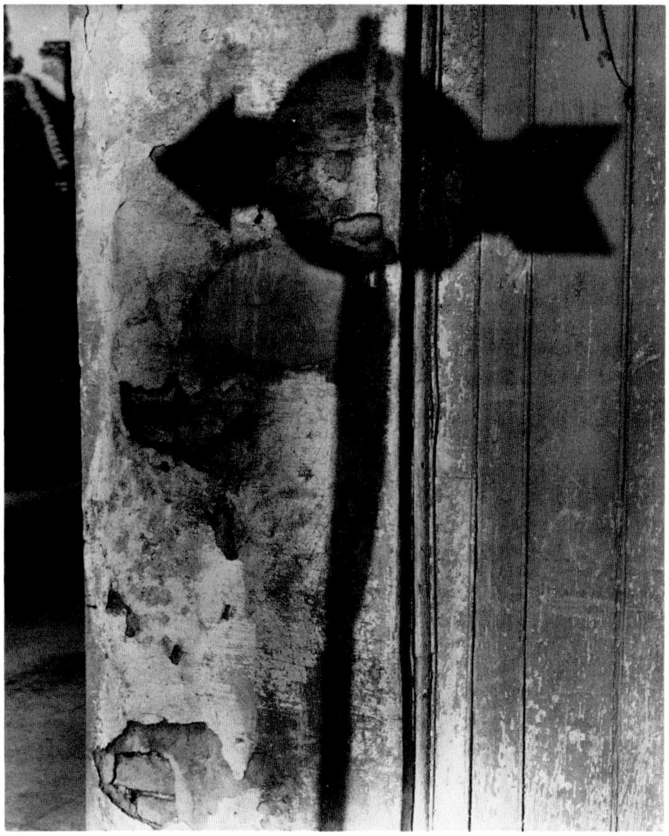

Clarence John Laughlin, *Figure Floating on its Own Reflection: 1957*

Clarence John Laughlin, *The Portent in the Shadow: 1954*

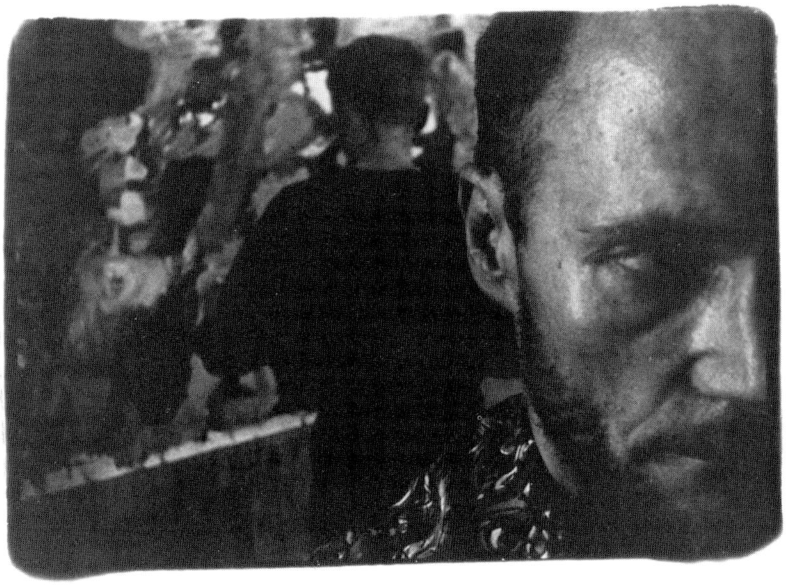

18 W. Eugene Smith, *Loft Inside (Self-Portrait) Texas*

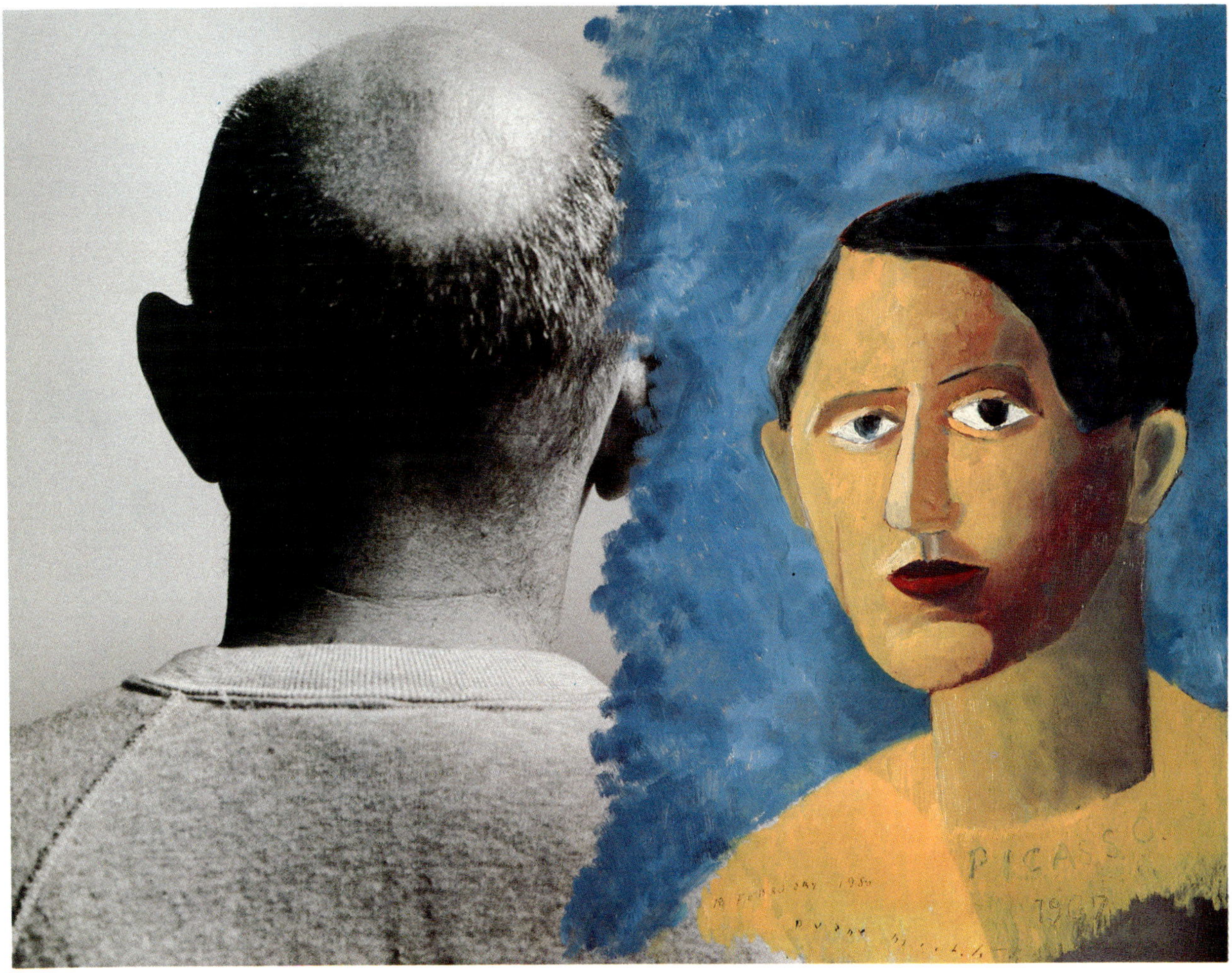

Duane Michals, *Self-Portrait 1979 with Pablo Picasso 1909*

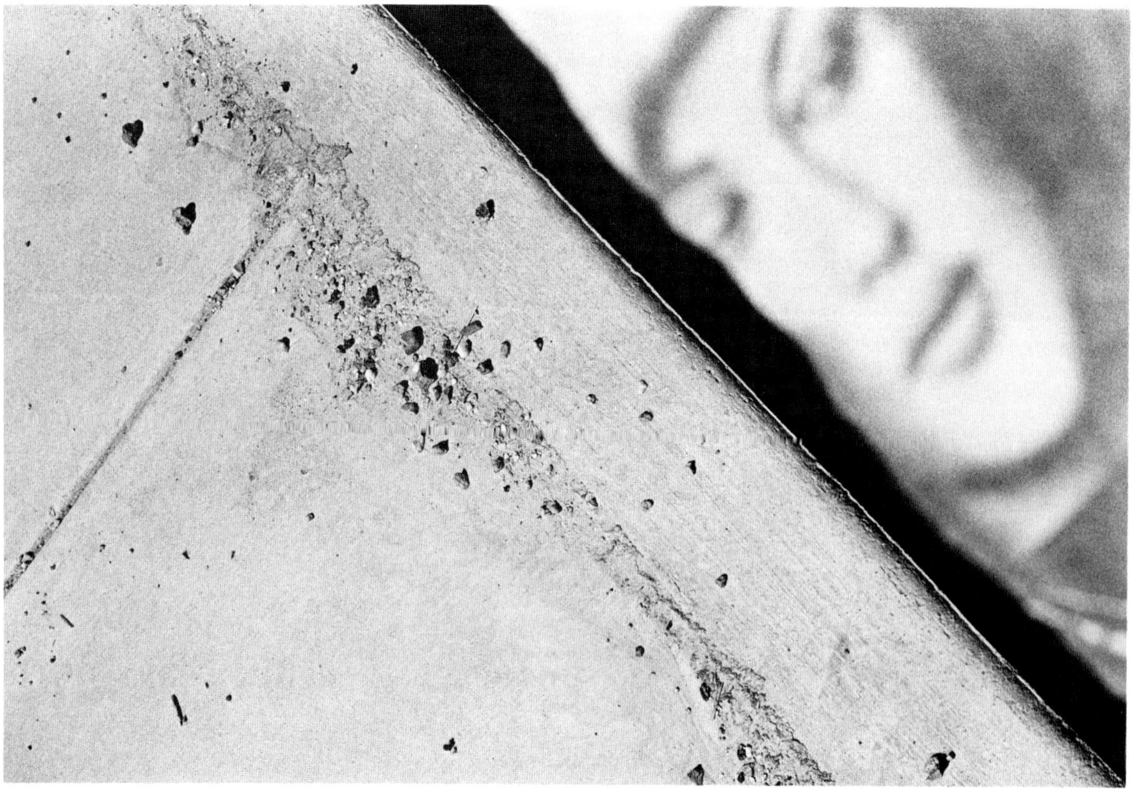

Ray K. Metzker, *Untitled from "Pictus Interruptus"*

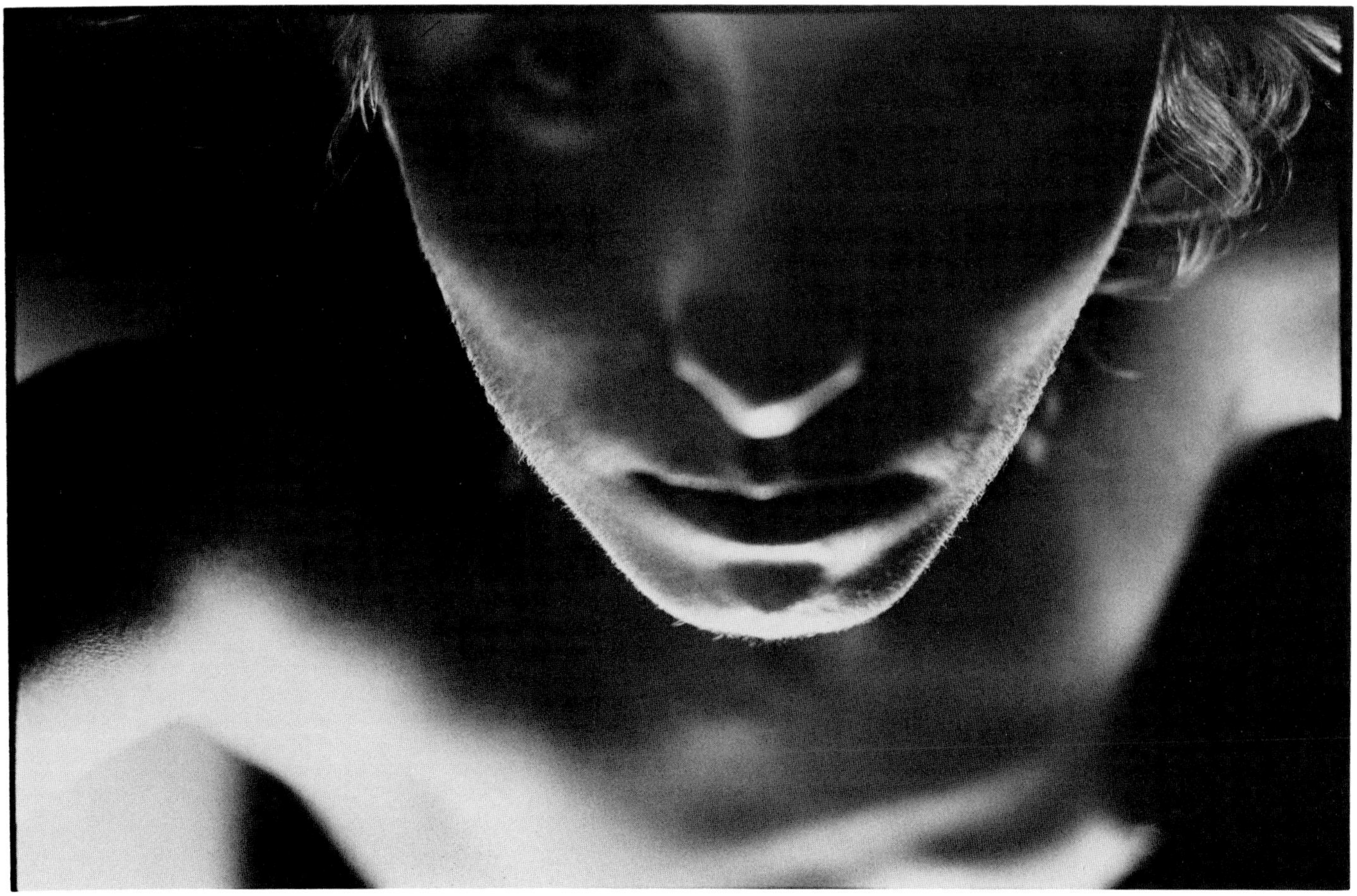

Elizabeth Turk, *Self-Portrait, 1979*

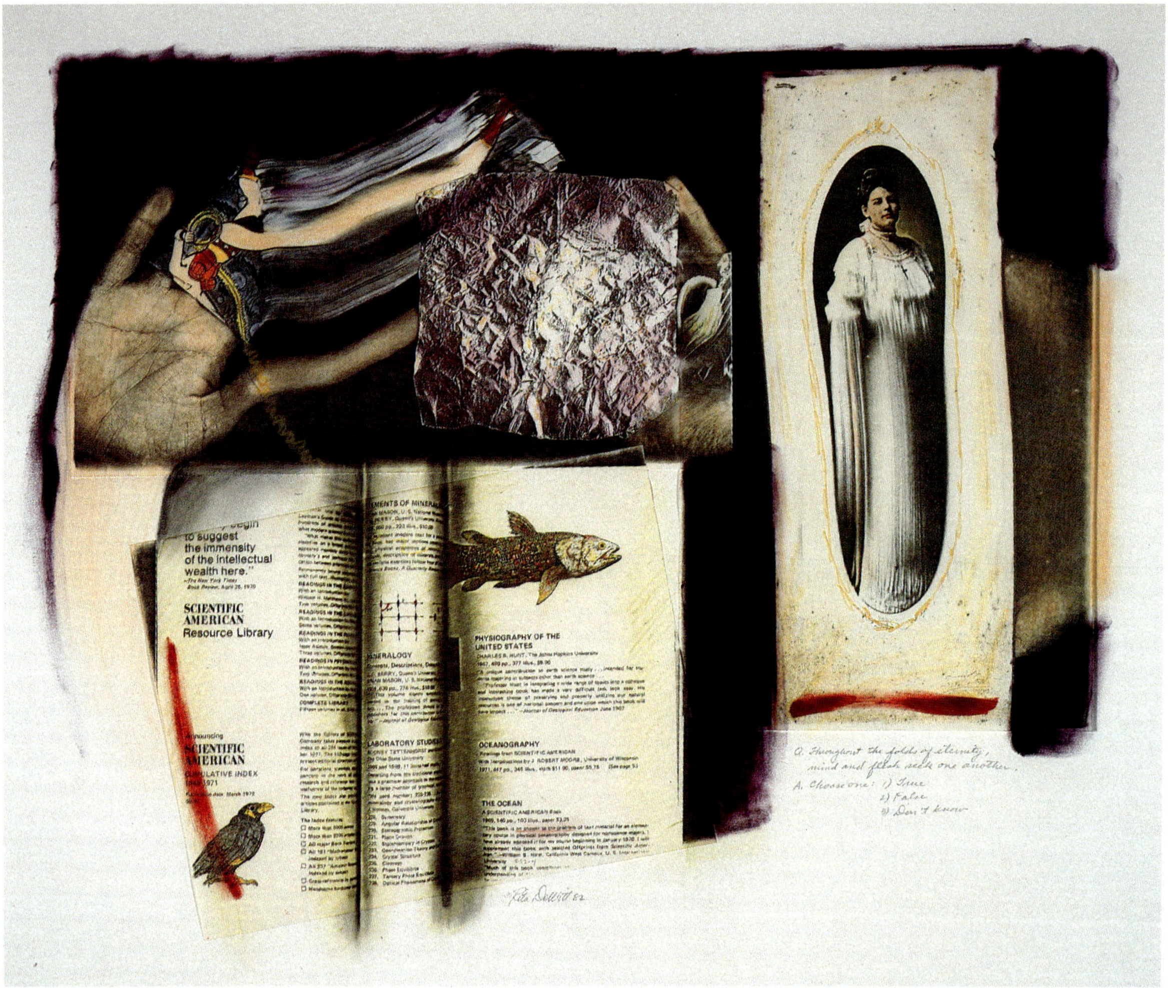

Rita DeWitt, *Q. Throughout the folds of eternity mind and flesh seek one another. A. Choose one: 1) True 2) False 3) Don't know*

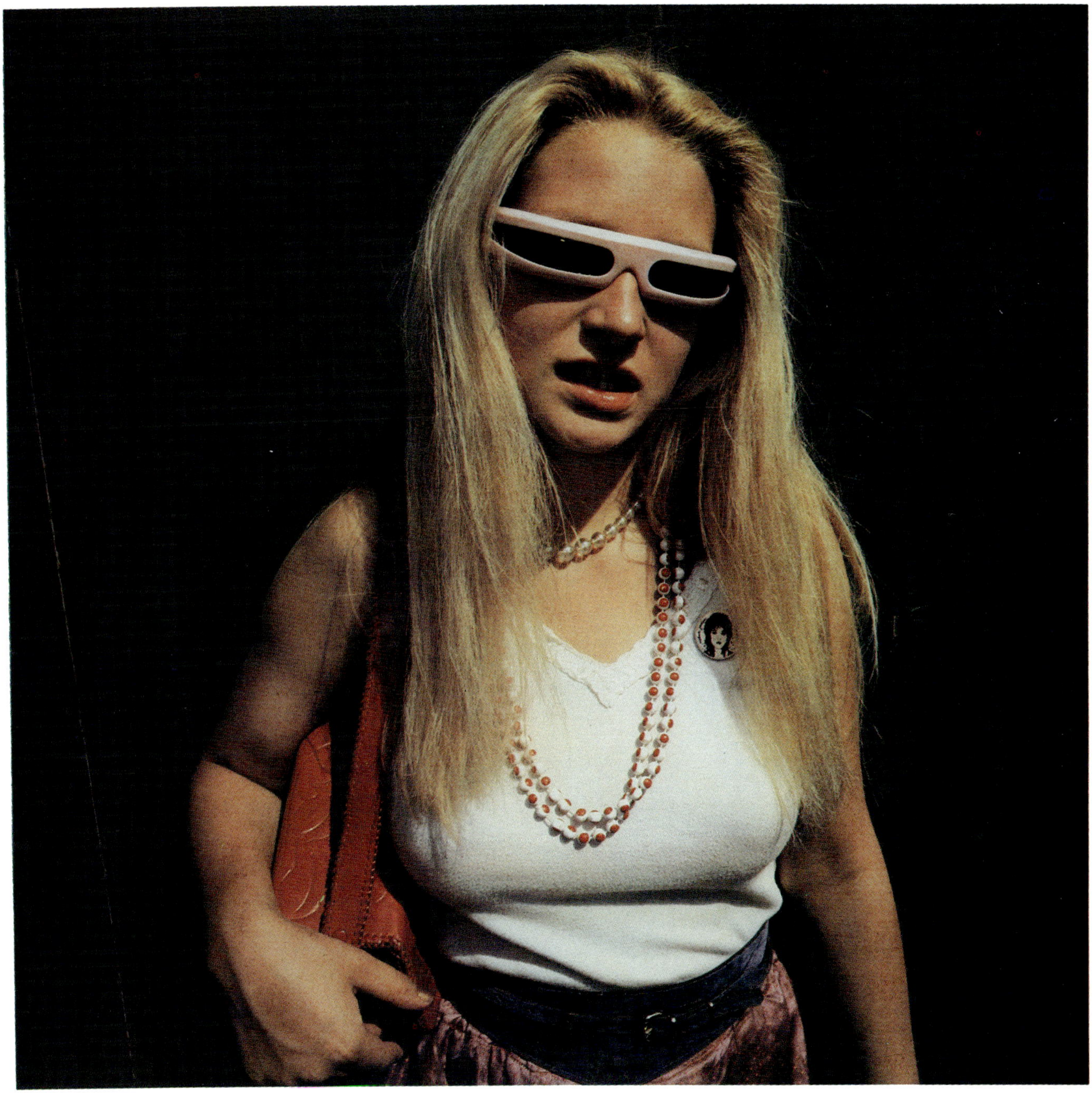

Stephen Livick, *Untitled, 1981*

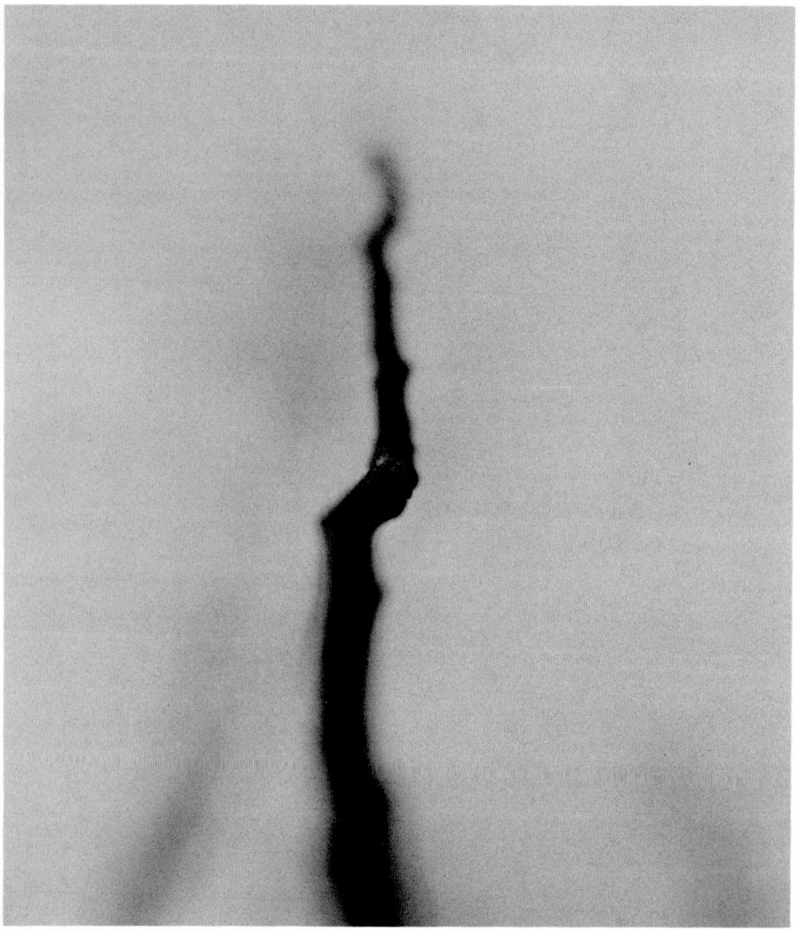

 Ralph Eugene Meatyard, *Untitled, 1961*

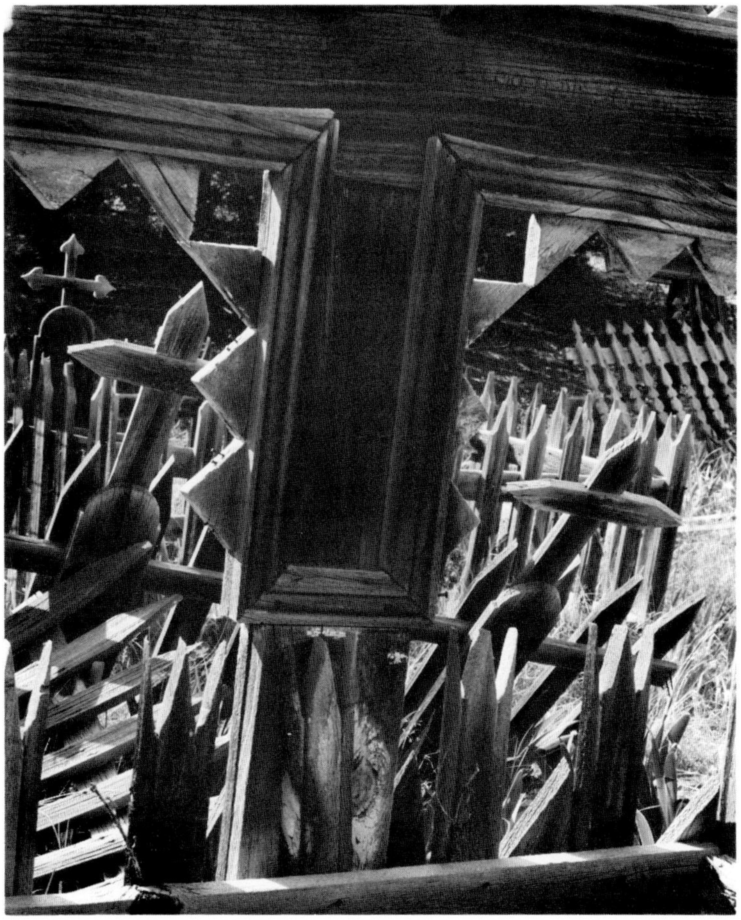

Laura Gilpin, *Campo Santo, 1961*

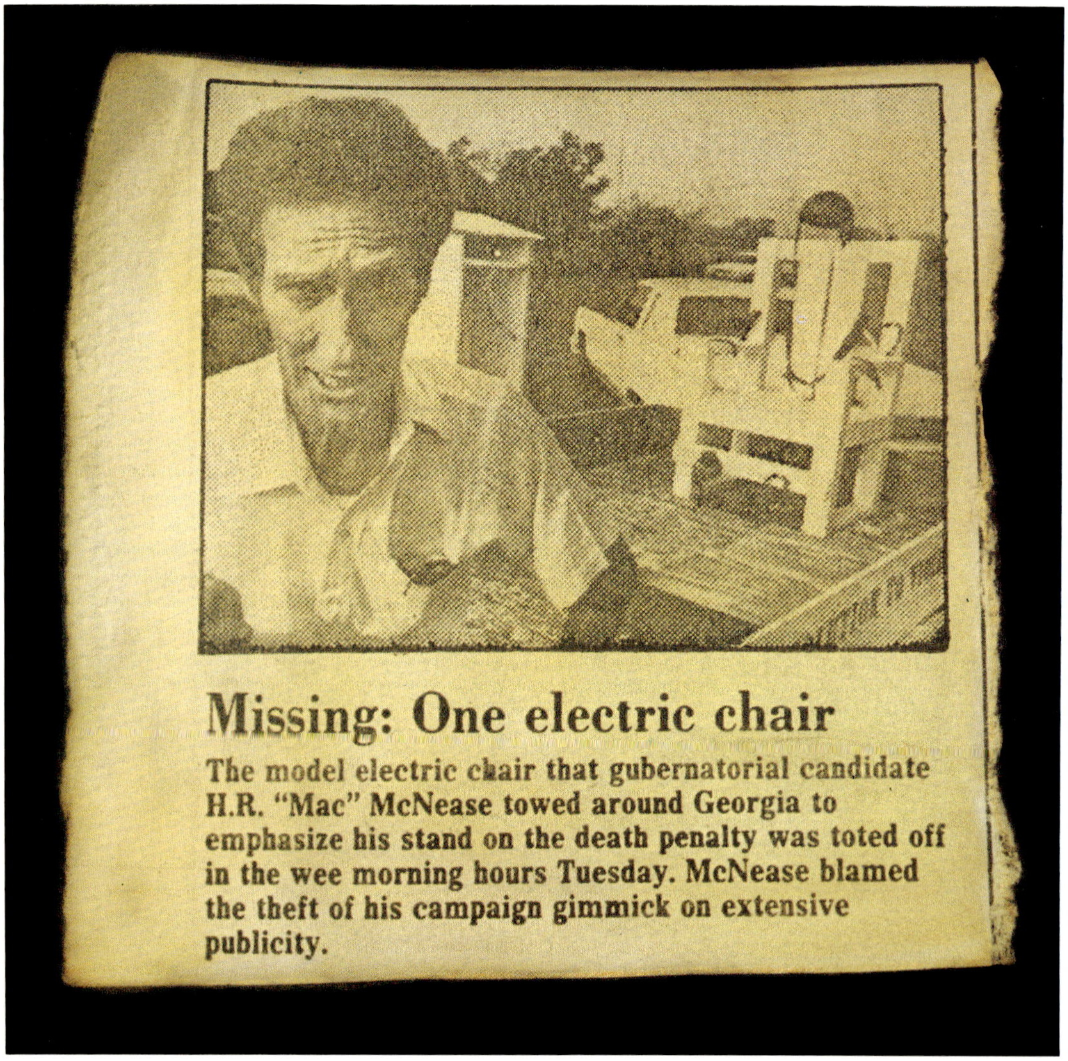

Missing: One electric chair

The model electric chair that gubernatorial candidate H.R. "Mac" McNease towed around Georgia to emphasize his stand on the death penalty was toted off in the wee morning hours Tuesday. McNease blamed the theft of his campaign gimmick on extensive publicity.

Virginia Warren Smith, *Missing: One Electric Chair, 1982*

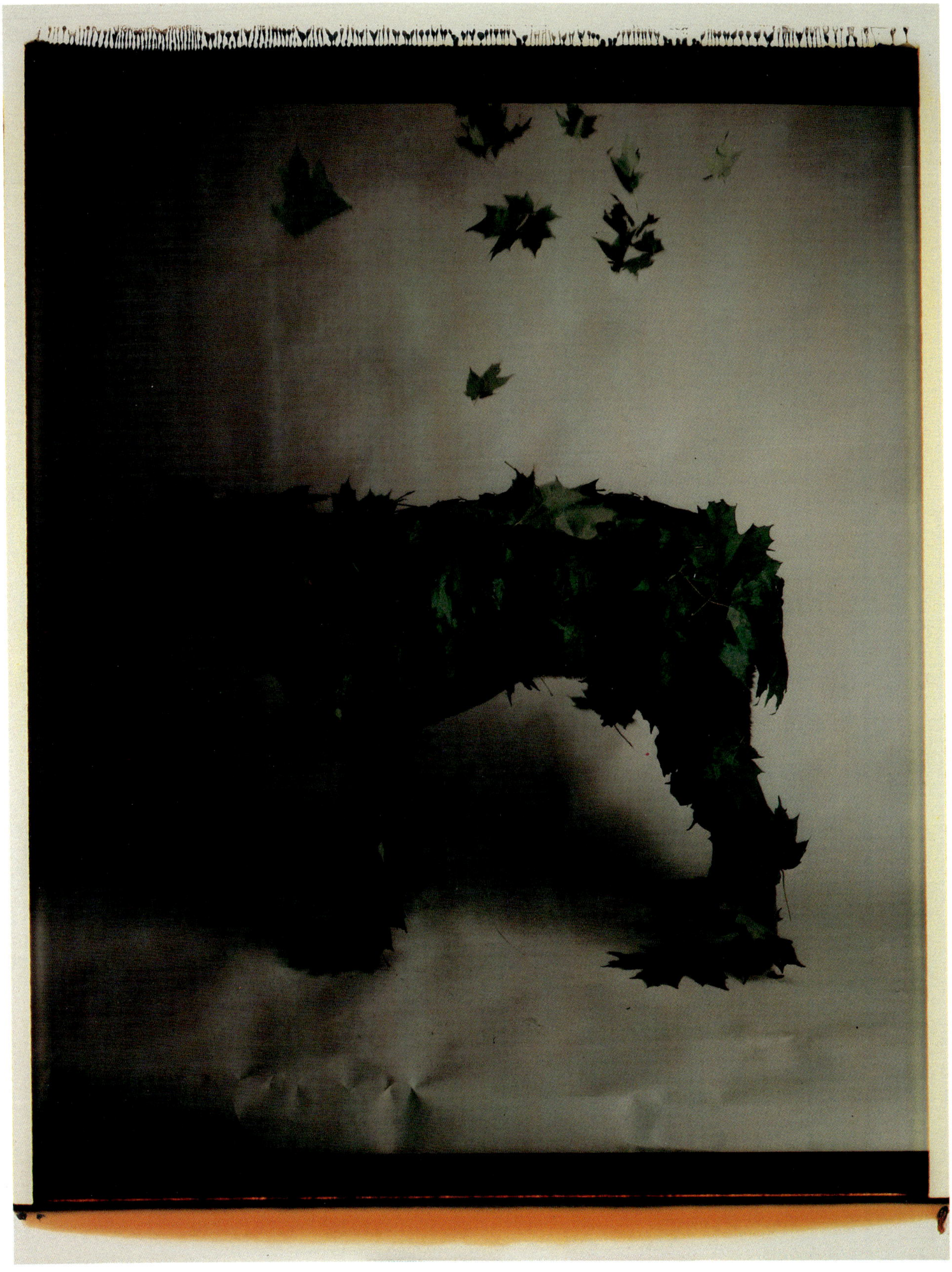

William Wegman, *Spring Maples*

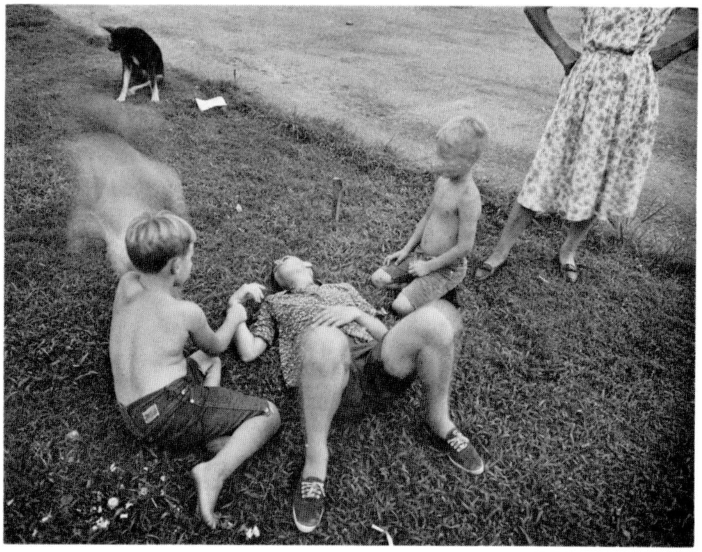

Emmet Gowin, *Family, Danville, Va.*

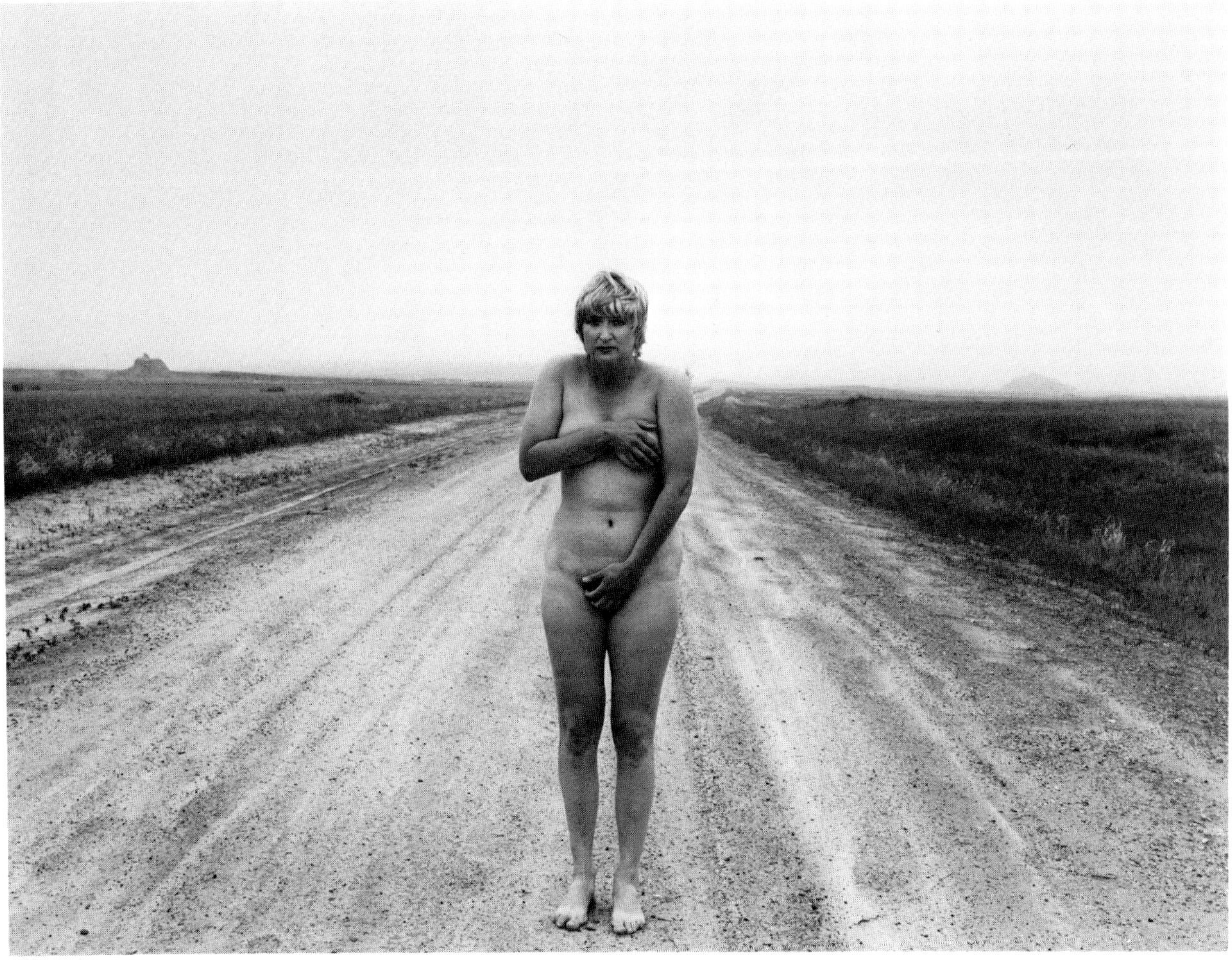

Judy Dater, *Self-Portrait on Deserted Road, 1982*

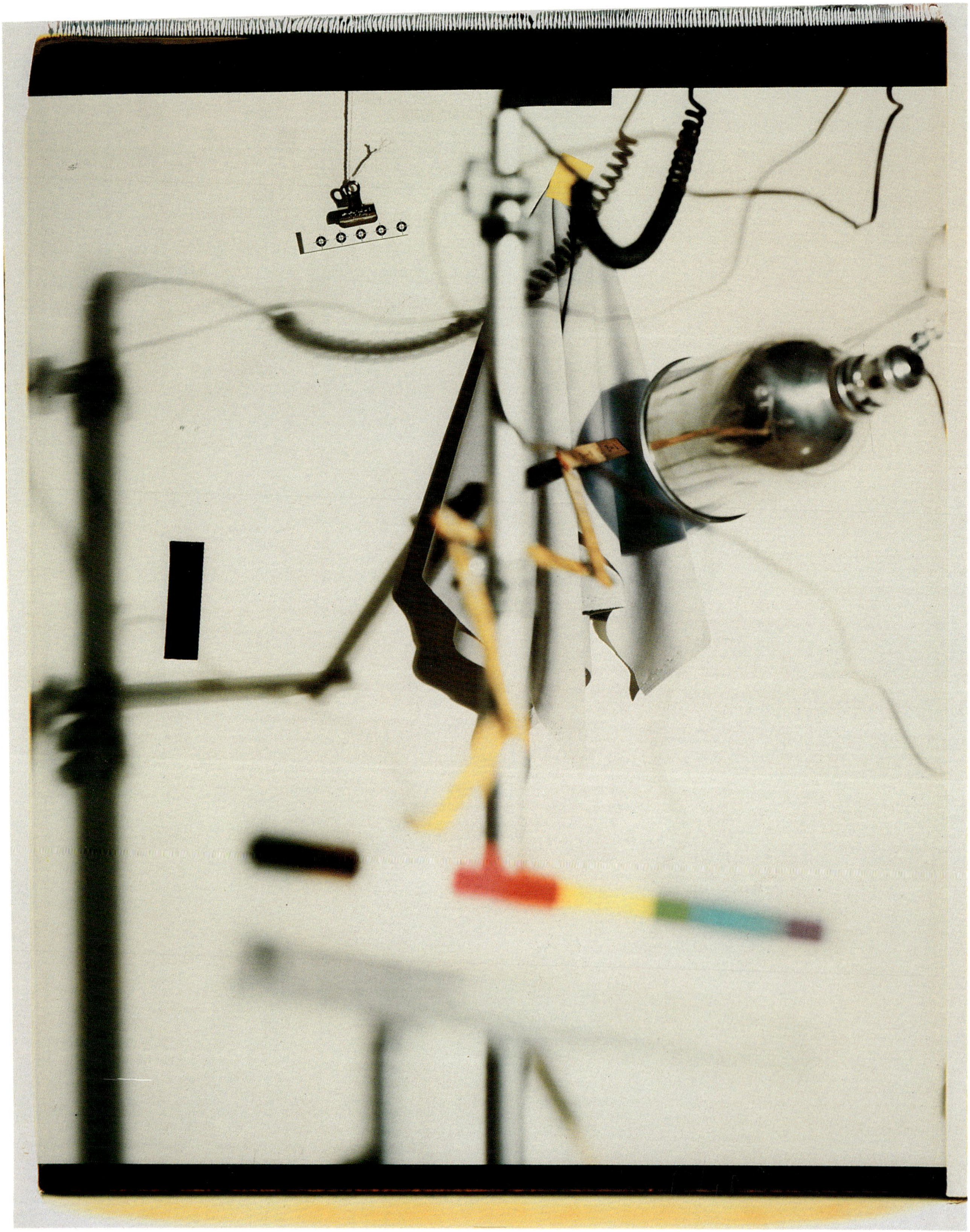

William Larson, *Untitled, 1979-80*

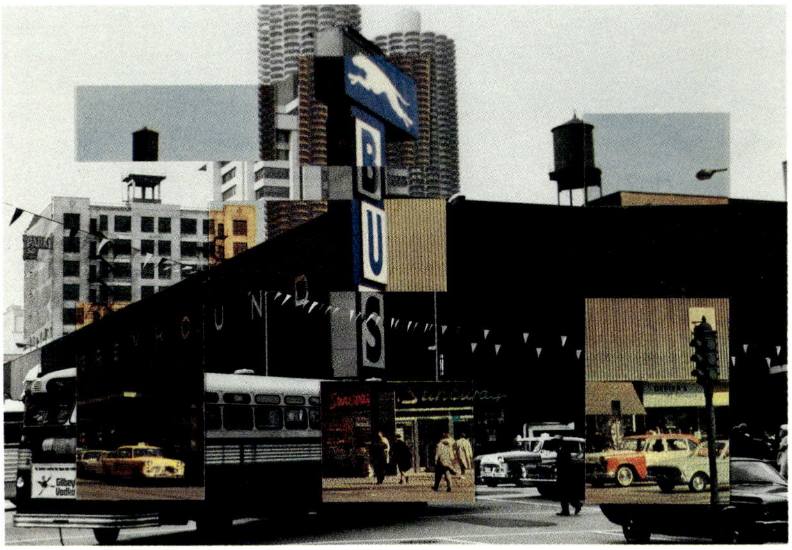

Ken Josephson, *Chicago, 1969*

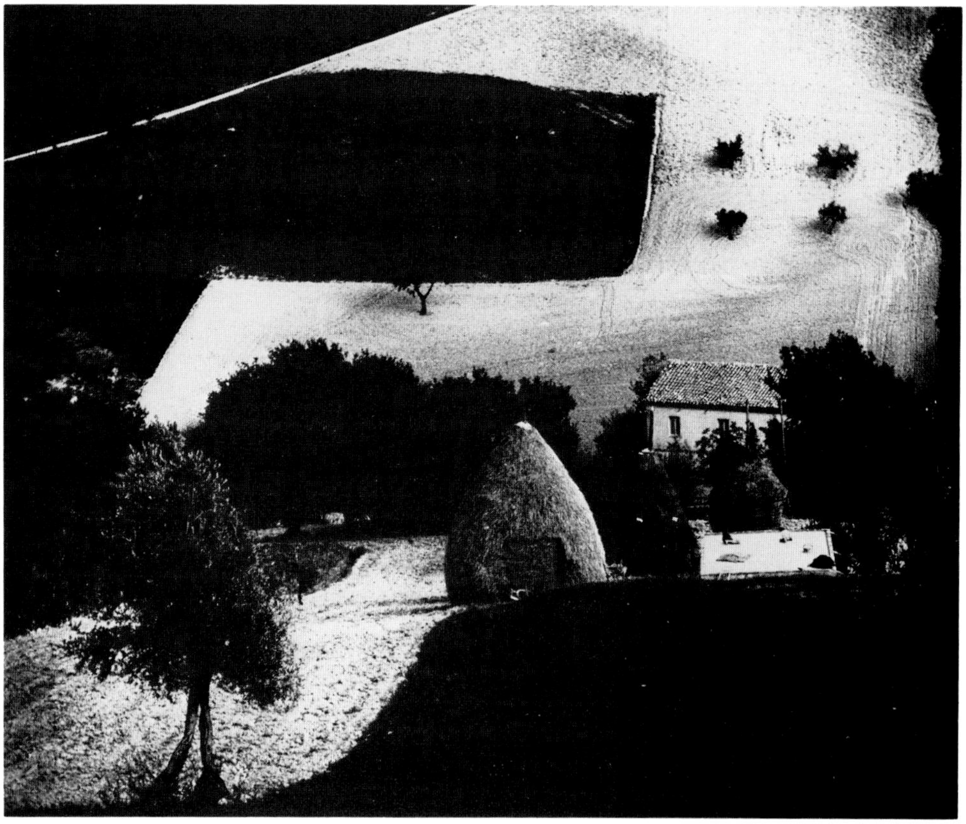

Mario Giacomelli, *Paesaggio No. 20, 1970*

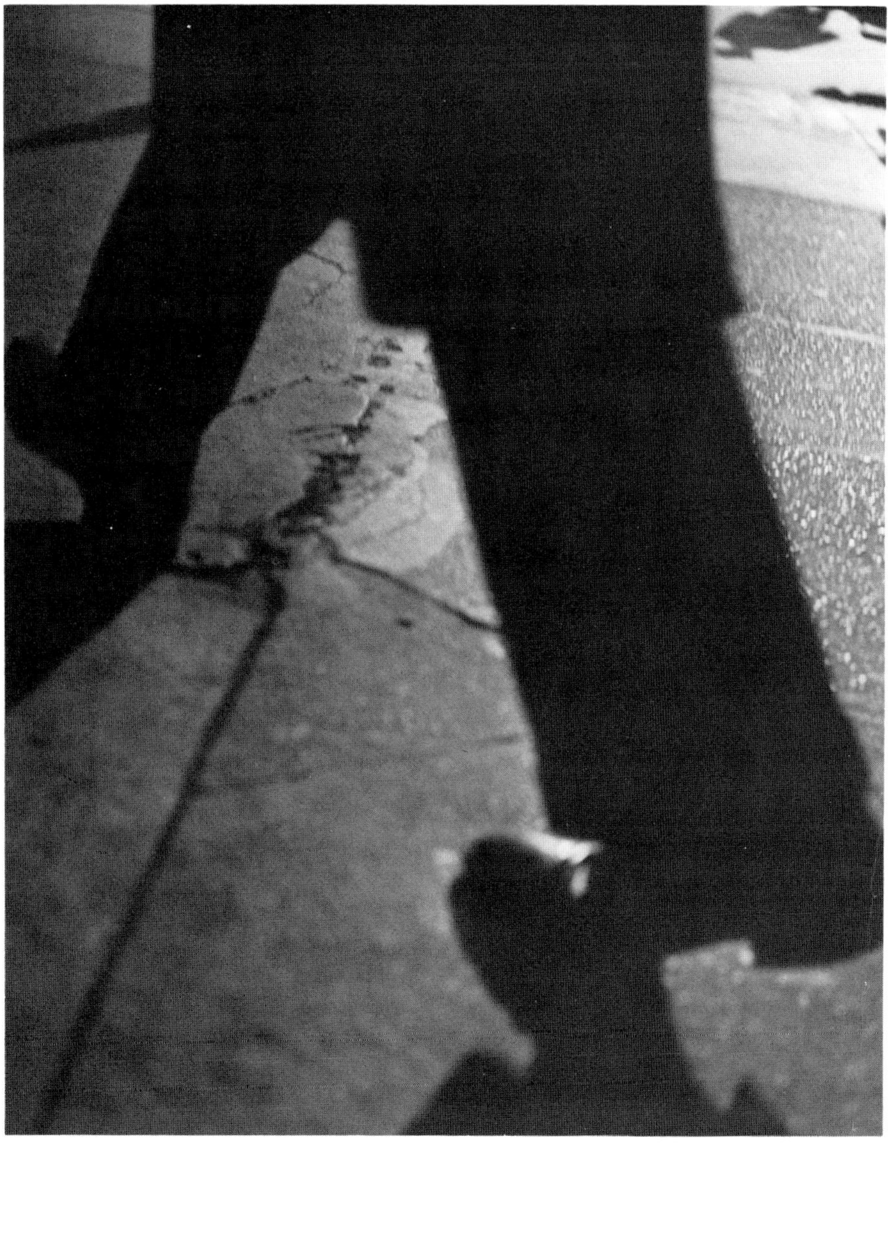

Lisette Model, *New York*

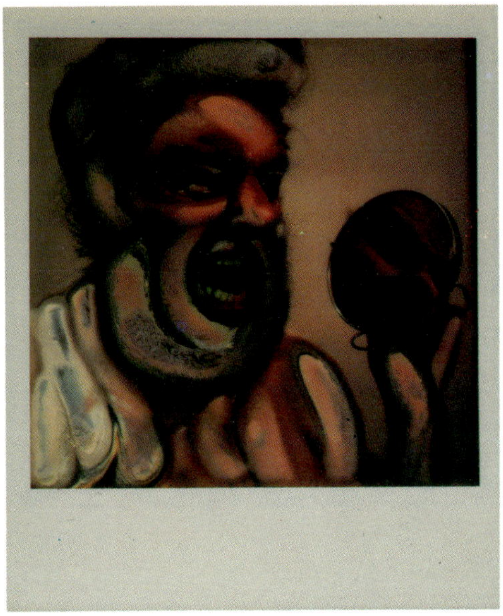

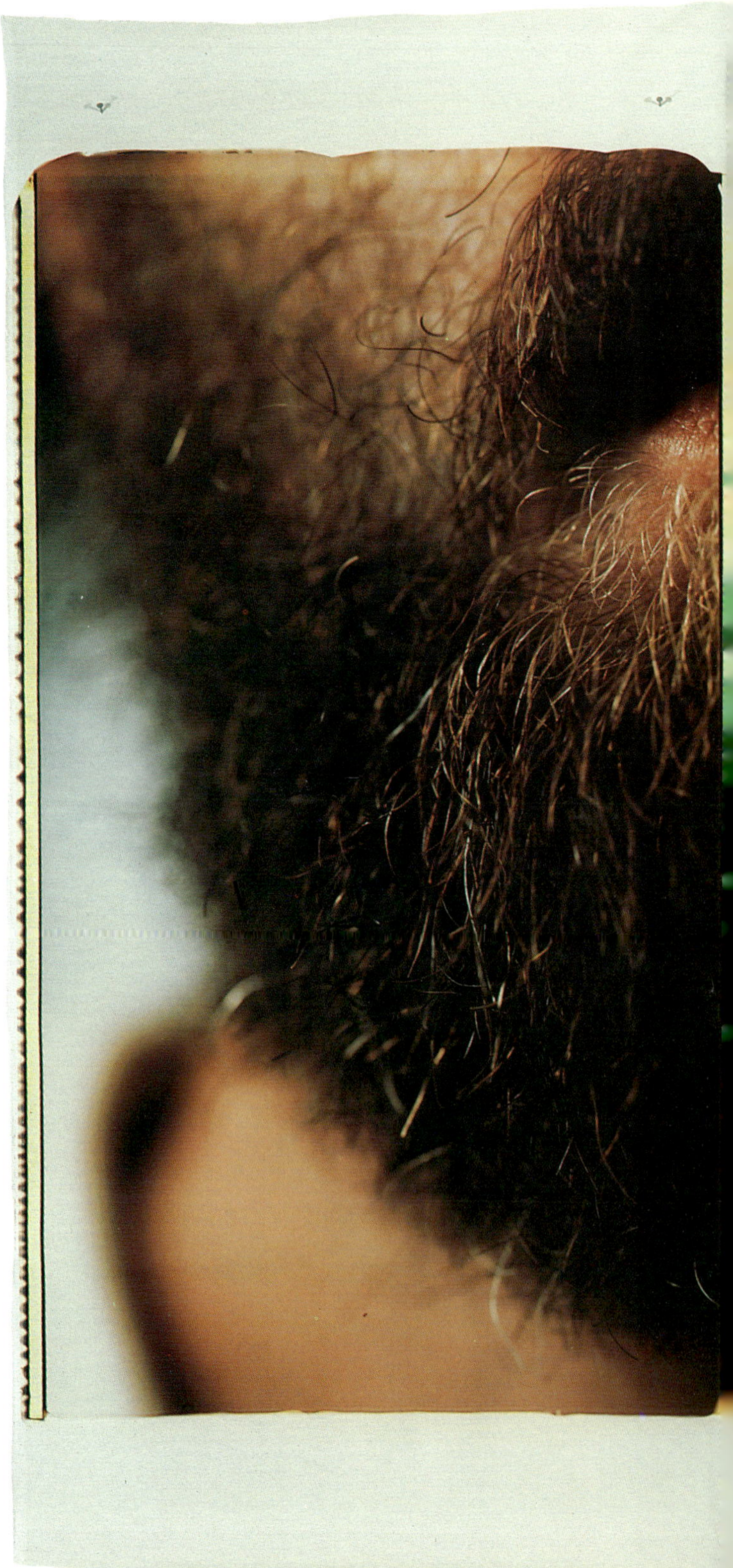

 Lucas Samaras, *Photo-Transformation*, *November 12, 1973*

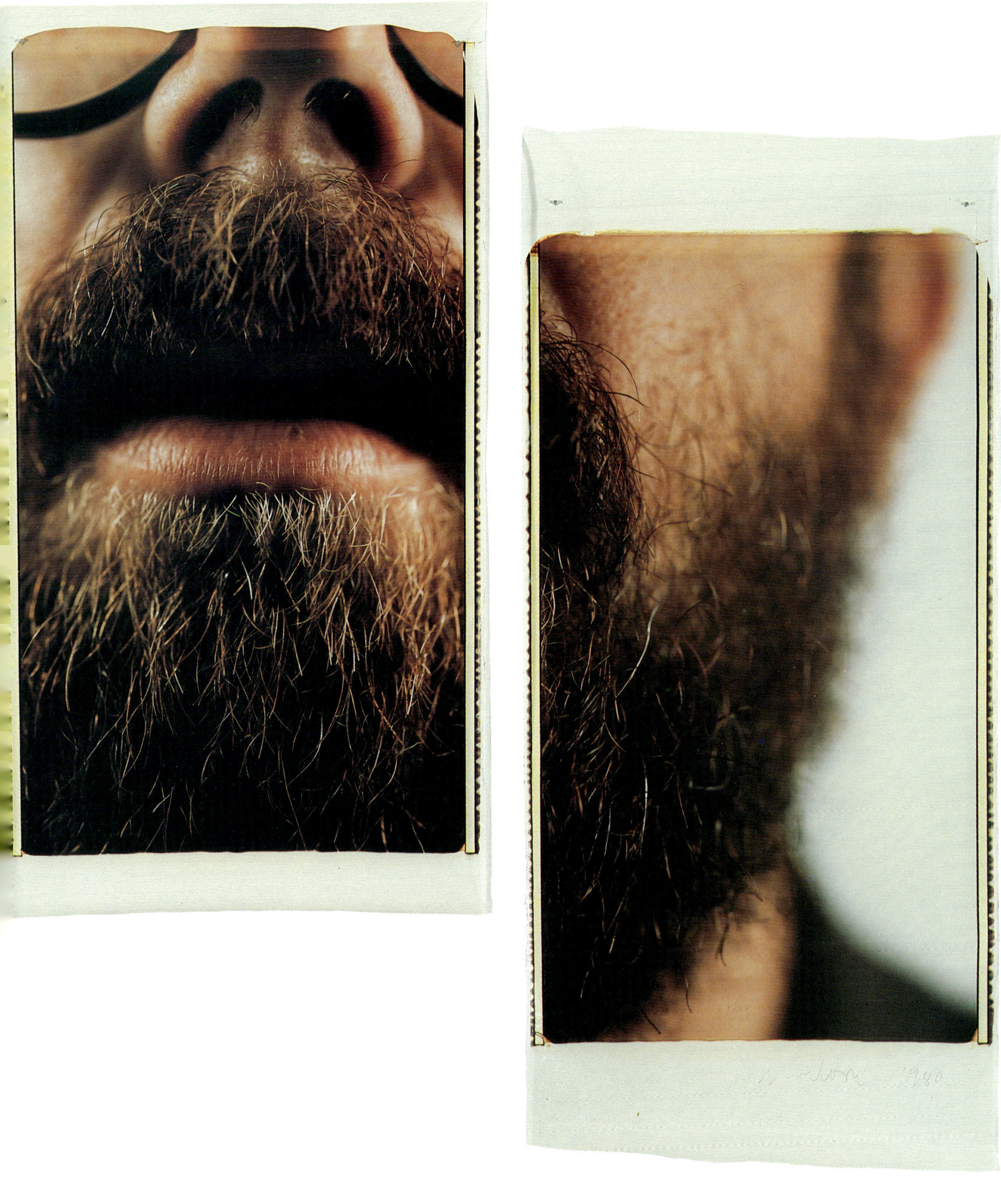

Chuck Close, *Self-Portrait (3 parts lower half)*

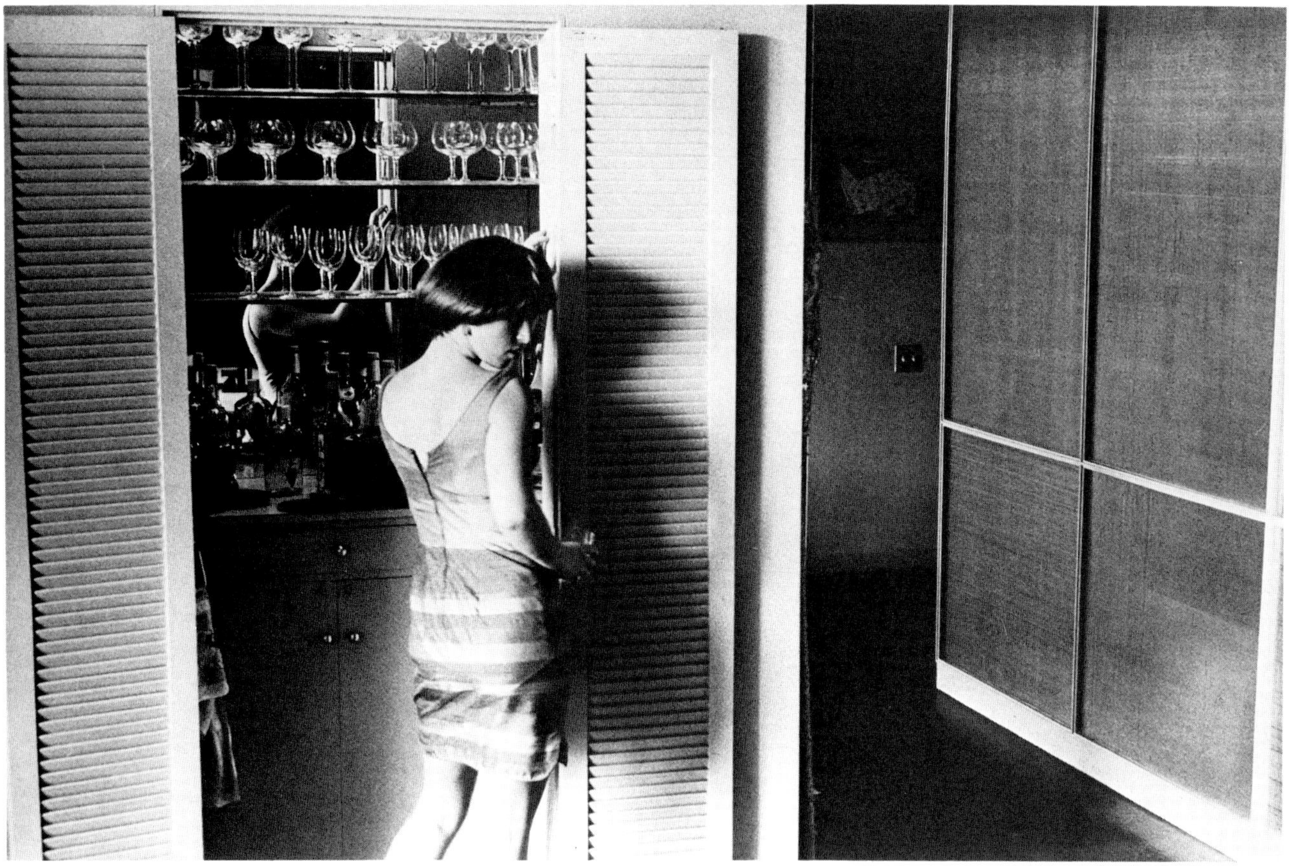

Cindy Sherman, *Untitled Film Still (Mirrored Bar-Phillips)*

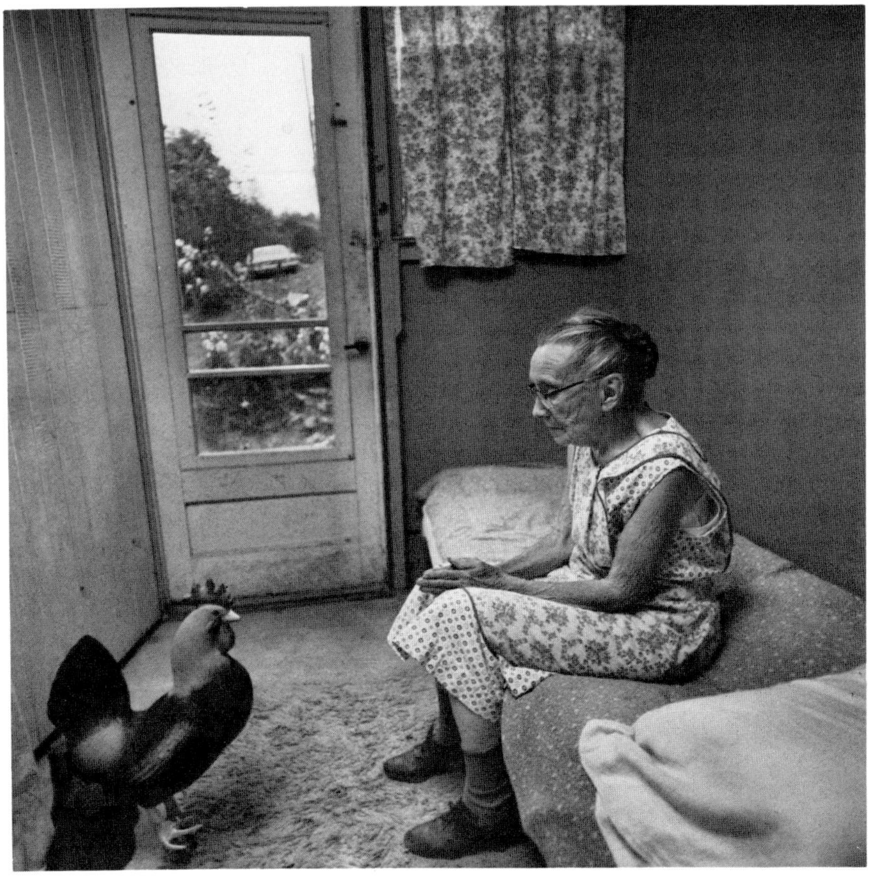

Arthur Tress, *Charlotte Olds, Freeville, NY*

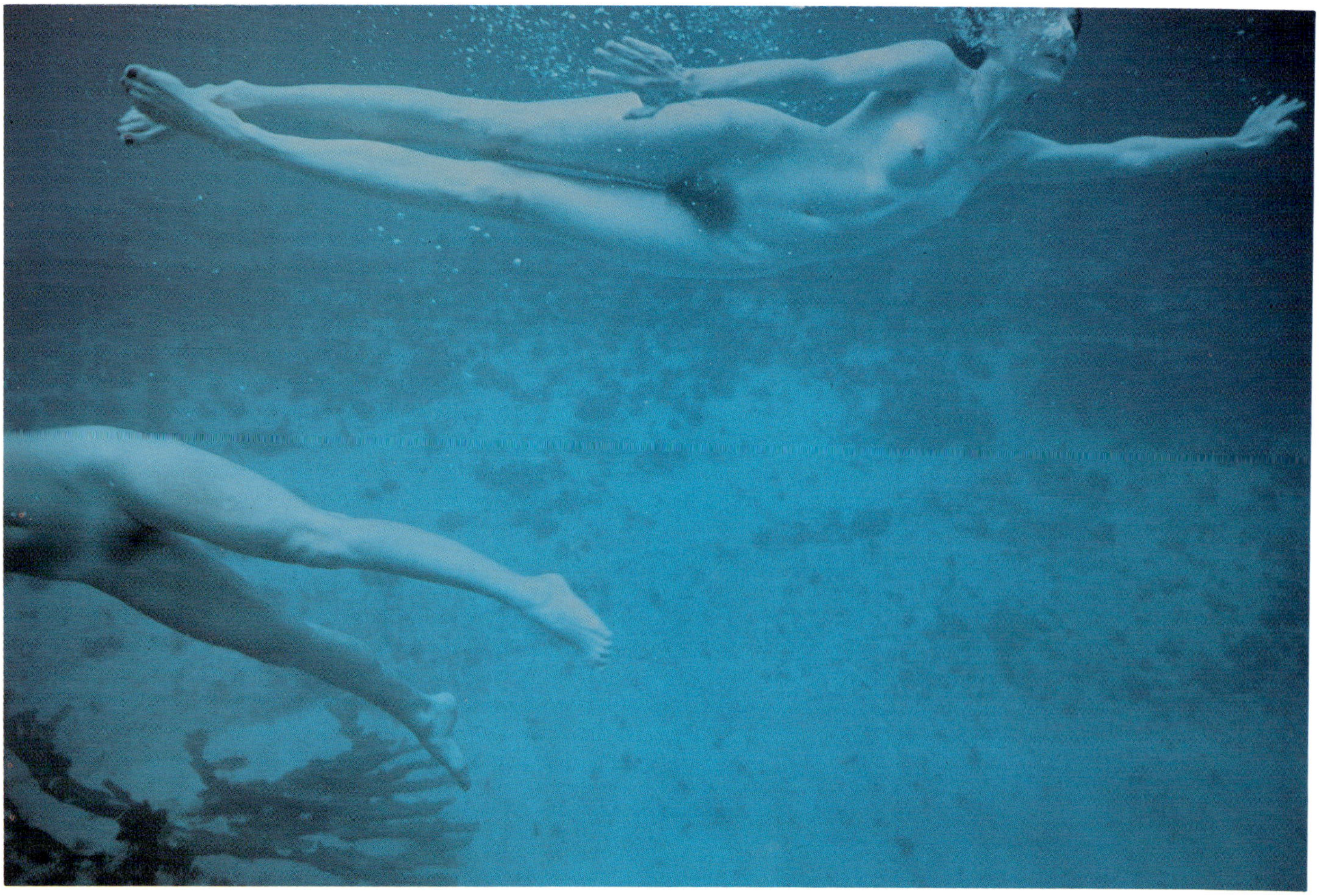

Laurel Simmons, *Calumny: Detail Truth, 1981*

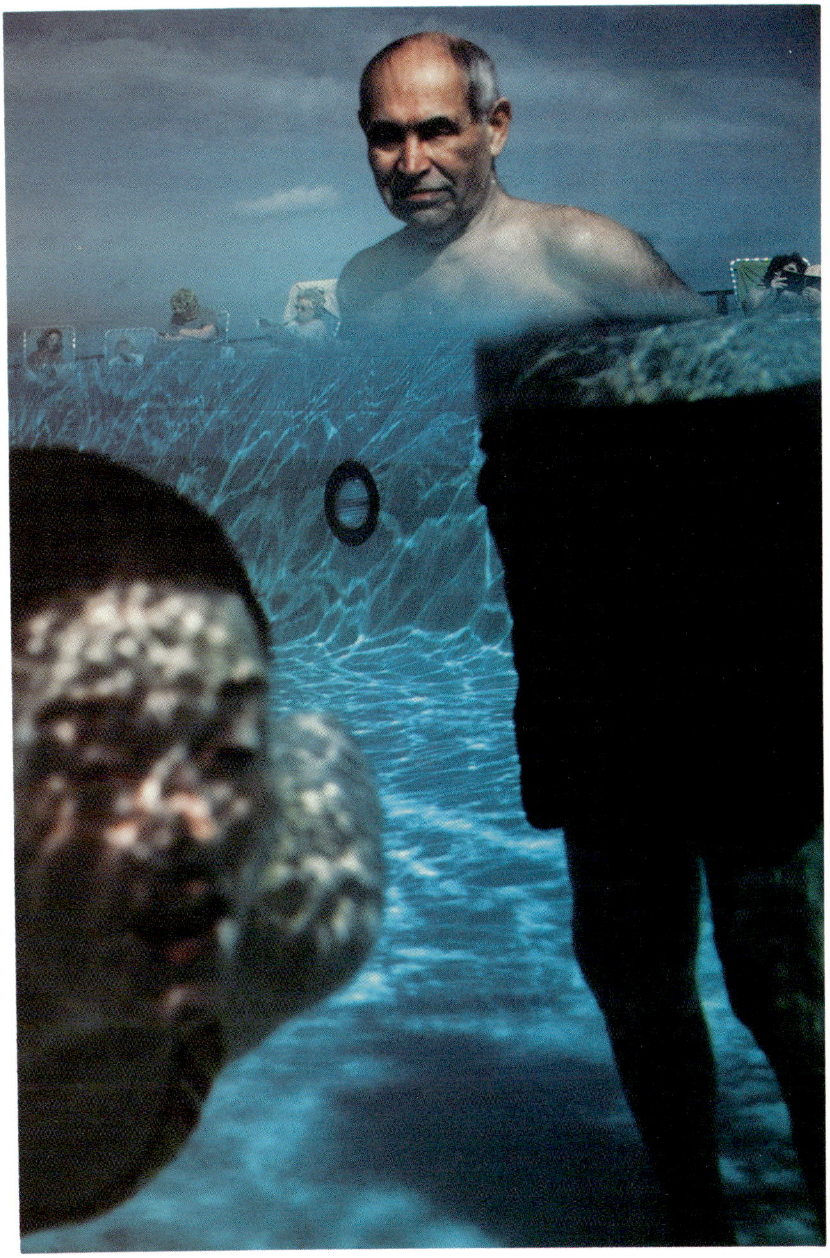

Jerry Gordon, *The Breakers Hotel, Palm Beach, Fla.*

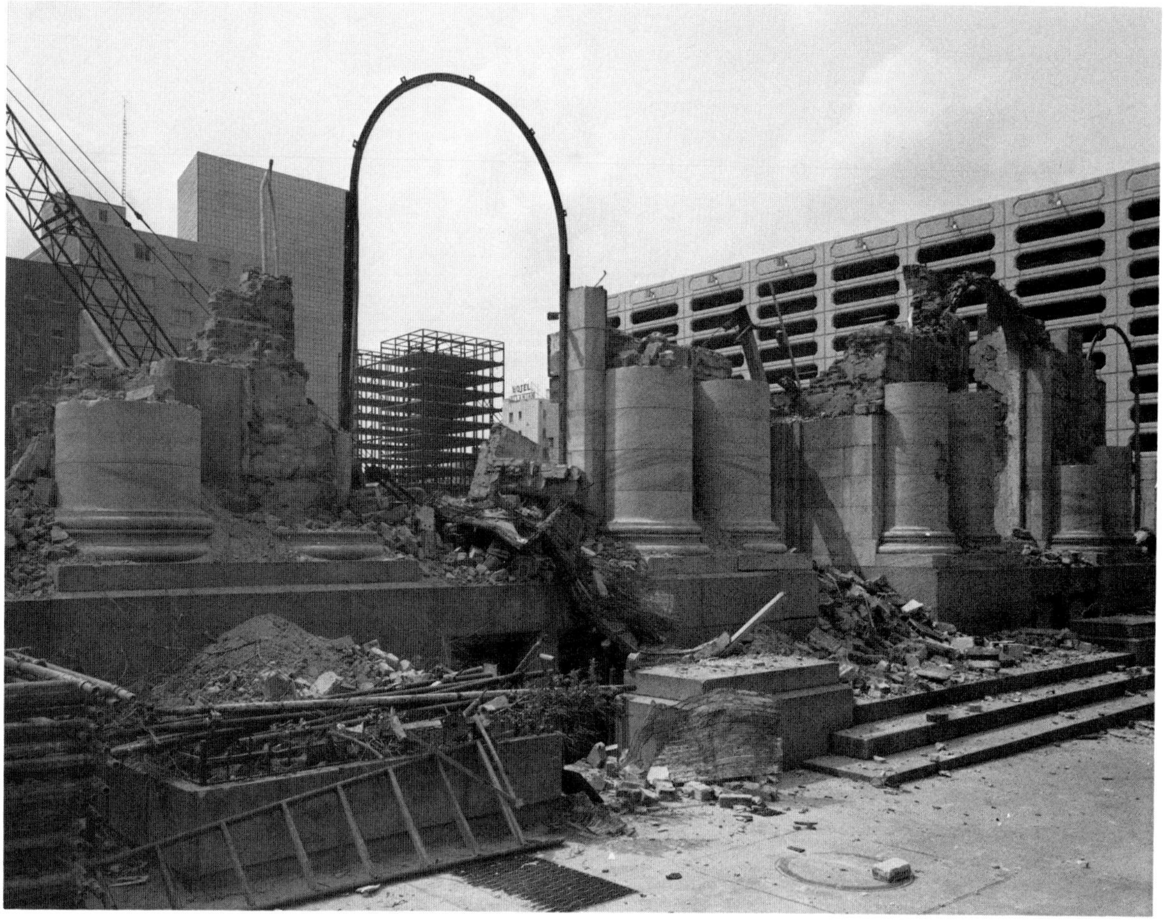

Martin Stupich, *Carnegie Library Demolition, Atlanta, Georgia, September, 1977*

SELF-PORTRAIT	SITUATION	PHOTOGRAPHER	PROBABLE RESULTS
Montclair, New Jersey (in front of a bus stop)	after traveling from up-state New York, dropping off a friend's car at her parent's house, 5 of us were waiting for a bus to take into New York City, some-where in the middle of Monclair, at a busy inter-section, a partly sunny day, cold, I was tired, and in a bad mood, it was time to take a photograph	myself, using an SX-70	good, I guess, I am stand-ing in front of the bus stop which is a covered concrete shelter, hand holding the camera which puts me in the foreground on the right side of the image, a cigar-ette in my mouth and a nasty expression on my face, Masumi Hayashi is in the middle ground under the shelter (she said she was looking away), I threw the print away before it developed

Robert B. Stewart, *Self-Portrait, Montclair, N.J., 1982*

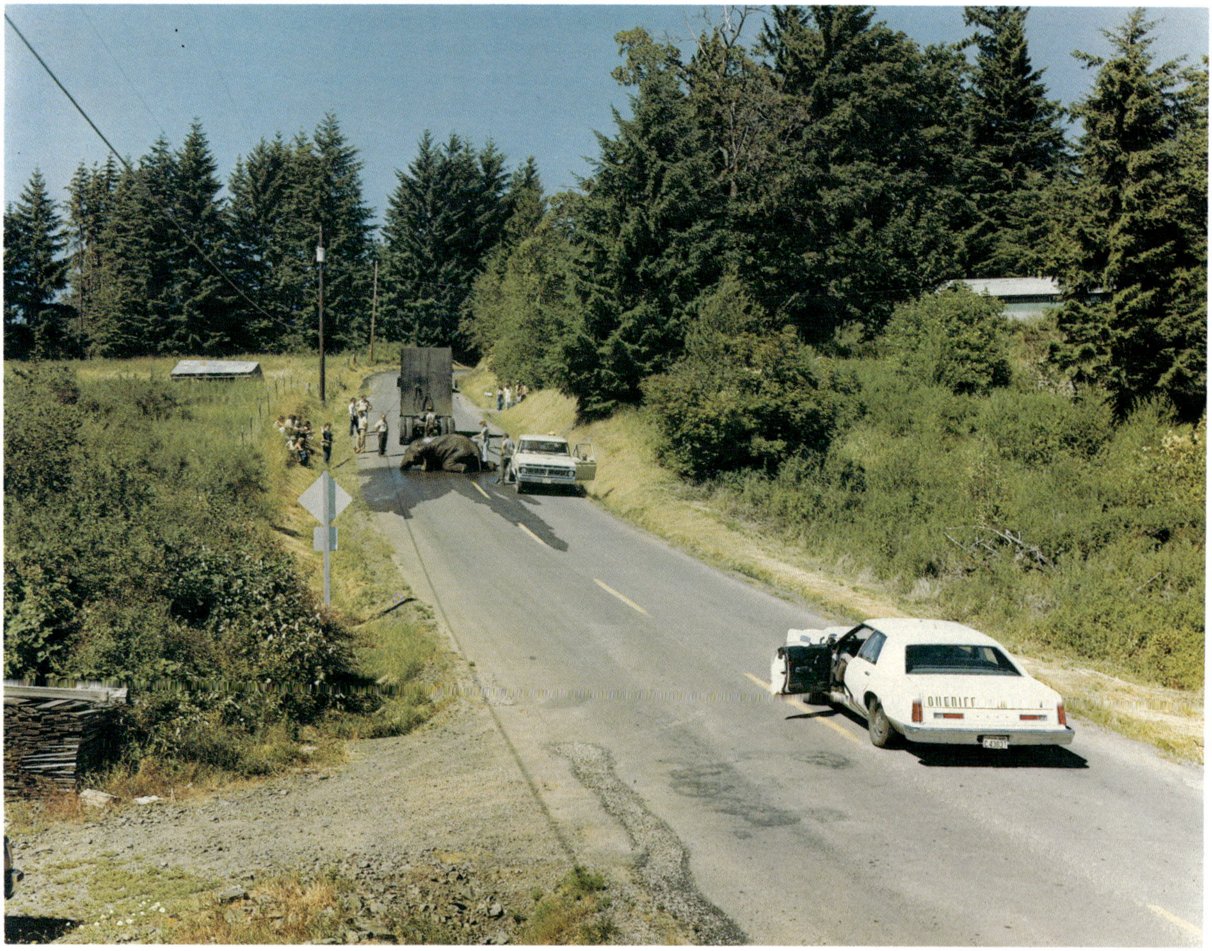

Joel Sternfeld, *Exhausted Renegade Elephant, Woodburn, Washington, June 1979*

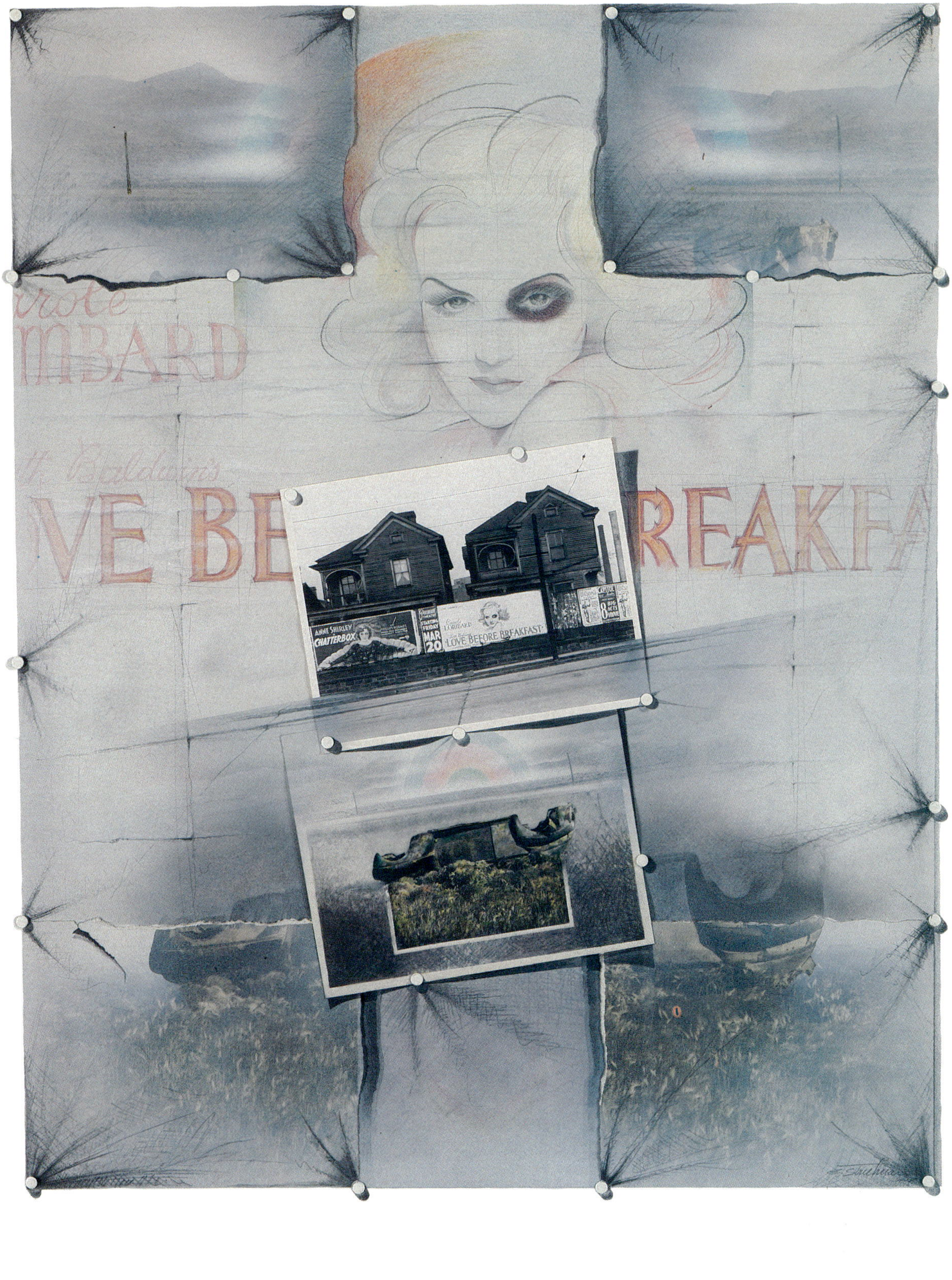

Evon Streetman, *Love Before Breakfast, 1981*

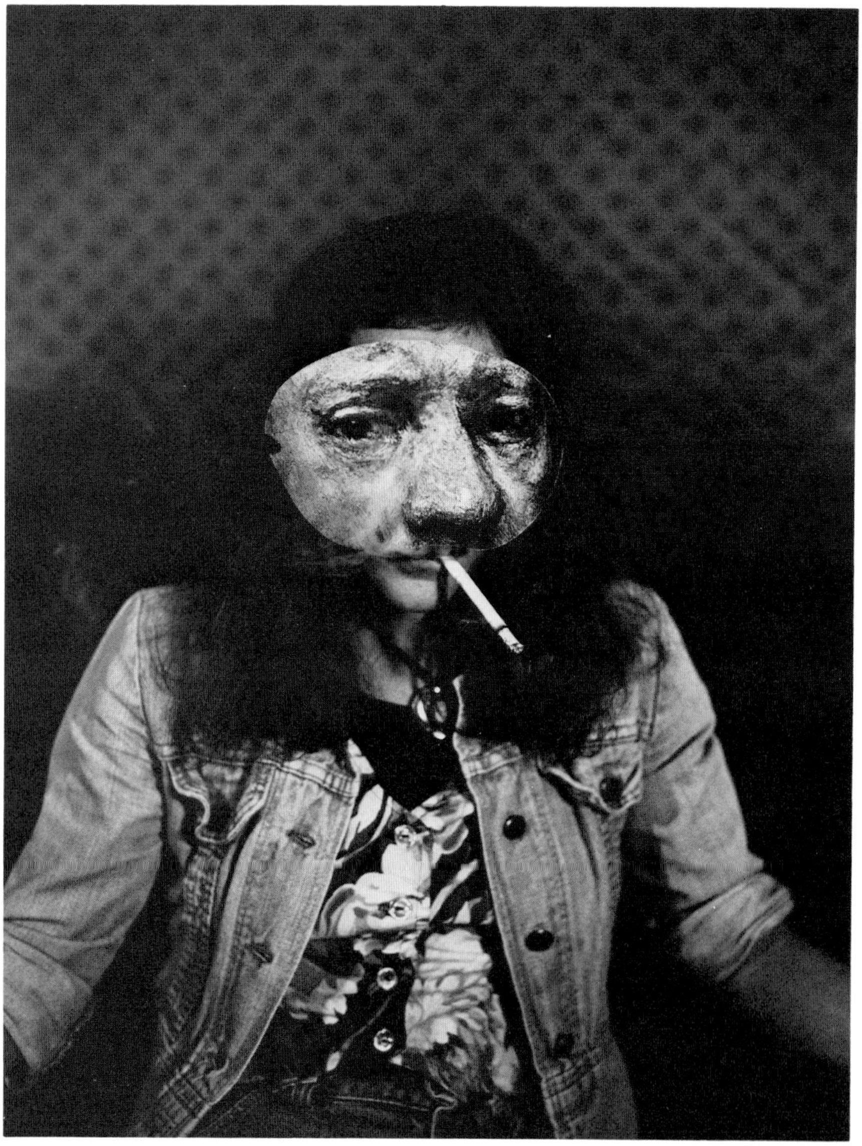

Richard Scott Hill, *Lyn–From the Rembrandt Mask Series, 1982*

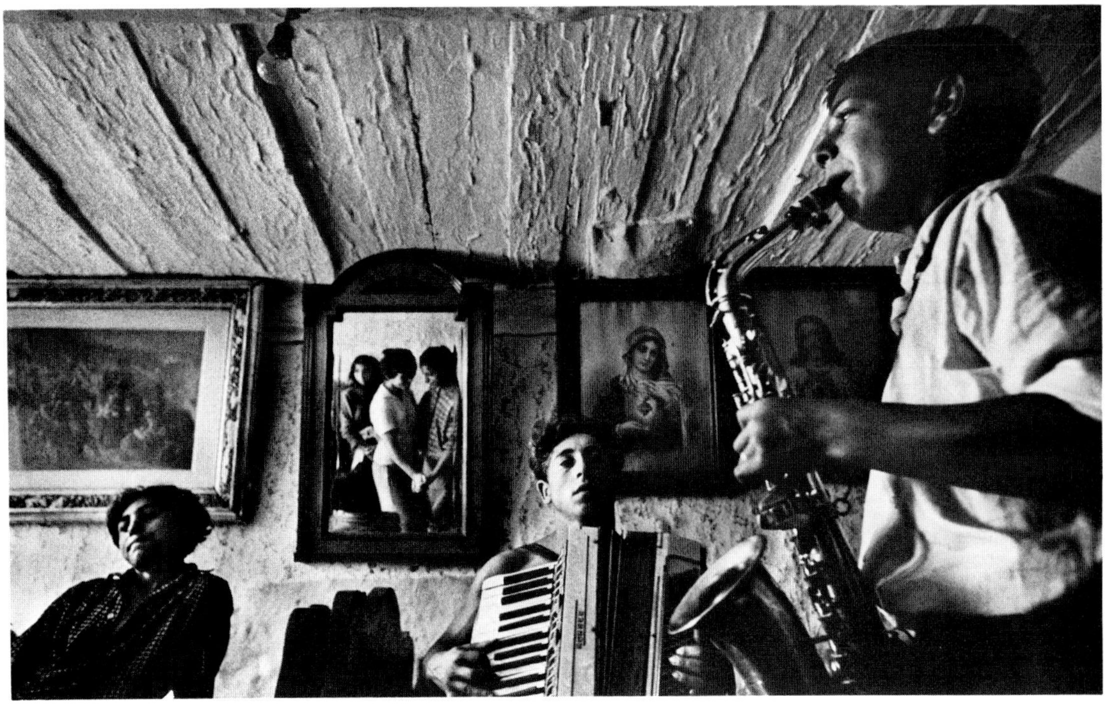

Josef Koudelka, *Velka Lomnica, 1963*

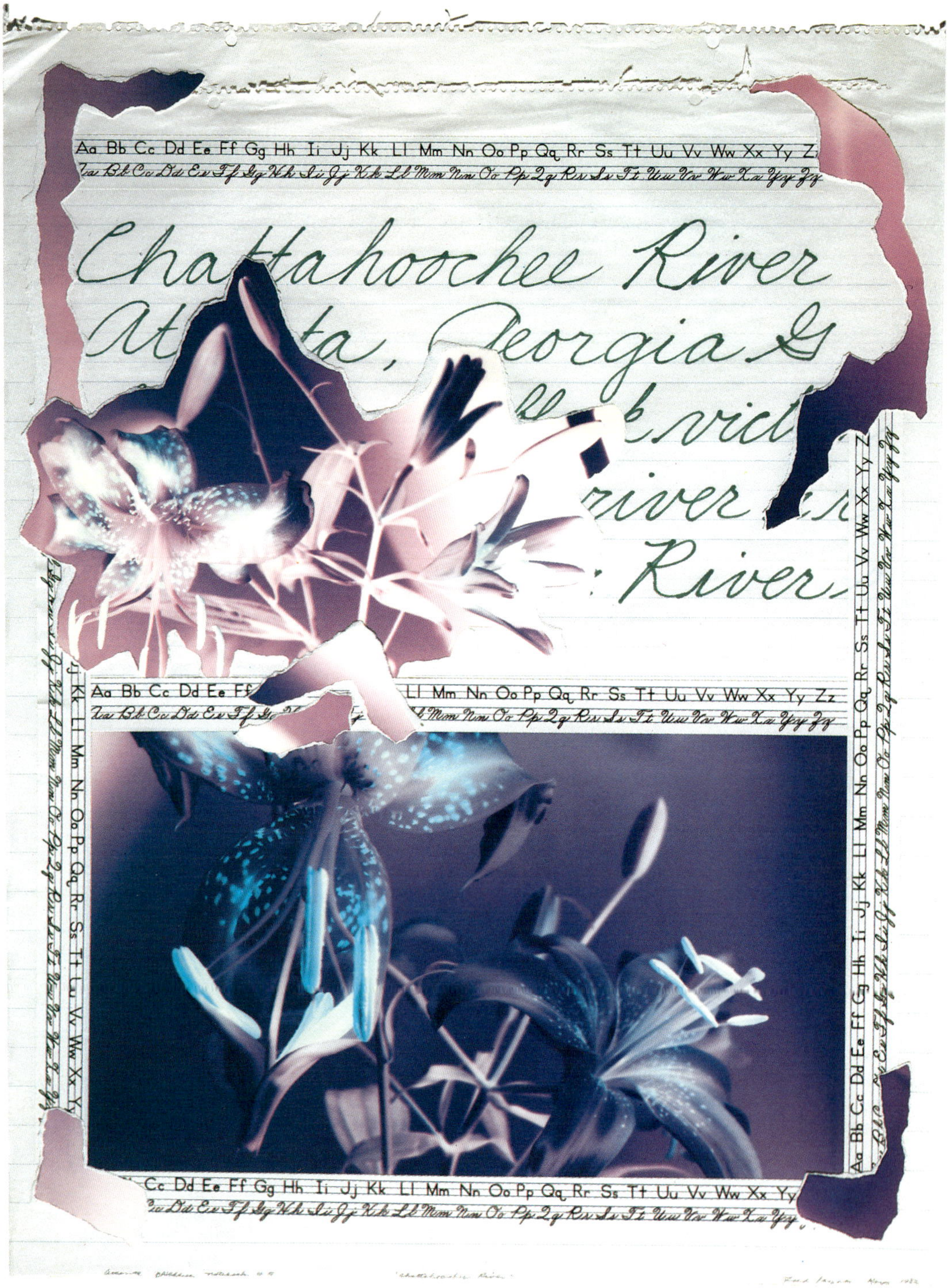

 Leah Jaynes Karp, *Chattahoochee River* from *Atlanta Children's Notebook*

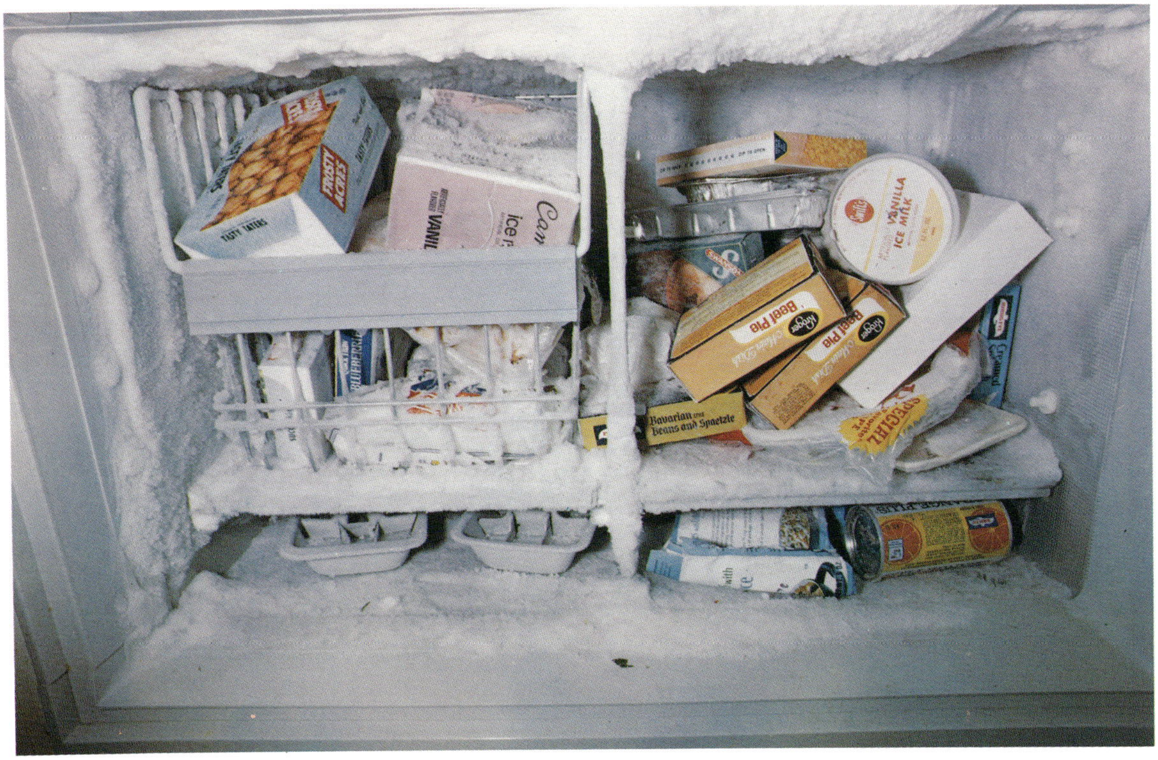

William Eggleston, *Untitled* (Freezer)

Clarence John Laughlin

Born 1905, Lake Charles, Louisiana
Lives in New Orleans

The Horse in the Witch Wood: 1948
gelatin-silver print
13½ x 10½ inches
1981.68
Not illustrated

Naturalistically, this is only part of the roots of a cypress tree found in a Louisiana *Marais* (or marsh). But through the magic of the camera when allied with the human imagination—it becomes a strange, and gentle little creature (with a kind of potato eye) such as only a child, perhaps, could have imagined. And this is evidence that the child's sense of wonder can be applied to photography as effectively as, for instance, Paul Klee applies it to painting. . .CJL

The Octopus Tree: 1951
gelatin-silver print
11 x 13¾ inches
1981.69
Not illustrated

This is one of seven photographs made of the same fallen tree—to prove that any photographer with an active imagination should be able to make a number of pictures of the same object—and in each image to bring out a new kind of meaning in the object. (There were 7 photographs made of this tree, over a period of time, and they were all published, eventually, in *Modern Photography Magazine* for September 1952, with a short article entitled, "Seven Ways of Looking at a Tree.") Here, the tree seems dragging itself along the ground—its form somewhat like a gigantic slain octopus (the portion at right forming the sac of the octopus)—this same portion will later be seen in a completely different way in *The Eye and the Dragon: 1951.* Aloft, a storm is rising. . . CJL

The Eye and the Dragon: 1951
gelatin-silver print
10¾ x 13⅝ inches
1981.70
Not illustrated

Approaching quite closely to the opening in the base of the tree (Cf. *The Octopus Tree: 1951*) we now see it as an eye socket (through which space stares) and the dried vines are like arteries leading to the living eye. Not only that—but there is a double image here—the right side of the socket forms the open jaws of a dragon—and at the upper right is a slit which is the dragon's eye. Here, then, in one image is a dual level of meaning. . . CJL

"Haveth Childers Everywhere": 1952
gelatin-silver print
13¾ x 10⅝ inches
1981.71
Illustrated on page 16

An arrangement with a piece of driftwood which suggests a striding creature with a sexual organ, a cardboard Victorian lady with movable arms and legs wide open, and some plastic miniature children. The title of the picture is from James Joyce, and the satire is on man's proclivity for random fertilization. CJL

The Florid Dress: 1941
gelatin-silver print
13½ x 10½ inches
1981.72
Not illustrated

The Florid Dress takes us to the simple whitewashed cabin, on a Louisiana bayou, of Mrs. Ida Turner, descendant of slaves. She is wearing a dress the floral pattern of which contrasts boldly with the sunlit wood. Below, hangs the chain to which the cow is usually tied, and the tub at which the pigs are fed—playing parts in the design of the picture, as they do in the life of Ida Turner herself. CJL

Poem at Noon (No. 1): 1940
gelatin-silver print
13½ x 10½ inches
1981.73
Not illustrated

A good example of how many of the prints in Group K (Visual Poems) should be "read" with the same kind of open imagination with which we read poems. Light coming at exactly the right angle gives this wall an amazing plasticity, and an almost eerie illumination. The lovely hand, even more luminous, accentuates the plasticity of the wall, with its circular movement. While in the dream-like black apparel, black on black can be discerned. CJL

The Elder Worship: 1949
gelatin-silver print
13⅝ x 10¾ inches
1981.74
Not illustrated

We are told that the most ancient form of religion was phallic worship. Perhaps it is because we have lost this relationship with our bodies that today we are so disturbed and frustrated. The Arched entrance of the church becomes the female symbol. And a figure emerges, as though darkness—the instinctual darkness within us—has taken a body, holding the ancient image which is rooted in the earthly cycles of birth and decay; the bearer of life, in a world of death. CJL

The Unborn: 1941
gelatin-silver print
13¾ x 10¾ inches
1981.75
Not illustrated

Against a background in which the feeling of barrenness is intensively conveyed, the figure—with her neurotic hand, and emotionally starved face—becomes a symbol of the many women in whom the desire for children has been defeated by conditions within our society. Note how the tiny head suggests both the head of an old man, and that of a child—expressing the unrealized promises of an unborn generation. CJL

House of the Past: 1947
gelatin-silver print
13⅞ x 10⅝ inches
1981.76
Not illustrated

Here, in this double exposure, are imaged those who are unable to face the realities of their time, with its tense and baffling problems. Seeking escape, they become trapped in the house of the past—rocking their lives away (metaphorically)—while confusion sits upon their heads, and they slowly turn into phantoms. (Figure of model here has visually melted away, and the picture is a transition from still photography to cinema. It might also be noted that many of the pictures in Group L (Poems of the Inner World) are actually visual notes for an experimental cinema which I have never had the time, or the money, to do.) CJL

Insect-Head Tombstone: 1953
gelatin-silver print
13⅝ x 10¾ inches
1981.77
Not illustrated

A memorial wreath made of aluminum foil, lace, ribbons, and carnations. It has an extraordinarily fantastic quality (probably because the subconscious mind is active in much of this rural folk art)—and suggests the head of a huge multi-eyed insect. (This picture was used as a cover for the May 1968 issue of *The Architectural Review*—London.) CJL

Solidity of Shadows: 1953
gelatin-silver print
10¾ x 13½ inches
1981.78
Illustrated on page 14

An overall view of a typical south Louisiana burial ground, where a multiplicity of plastered brick forms rises from the marshy earth, and where a kind of folk art can be found which is unlike anything in the U.S. (See *The Insect-Headed Tombstones: 1953*, etc.) Now, however, the intense shadows become more solid than the physical forms which create them; and the ambiguous distinction between "solid" and "non-solid" becomes manifest—as well as something of the enigmatic connotations of the nature of reality itself. CJL

The Enshadowed Pillars (No. 4): 1946
gelatin-silver print
10¾ x 13½ inches
1981.79
Not illustrated

(Chretian Point Plantation) This is one of the most significant of all the houses that link the Louisiana Colonial period to the later "Classic" period, in that it embodies features peculiar to both periods. The walls and columns are of plastered brick; there are central halls on both floors; the hipped roof was originally of shingles; and the house still had its wooden gutters (instead of the later metal gutters) when this picture was made. At that time, too, the inhabitants were still using the buggy shown at right. CJL

And Tell of Time. . .Cobwebbed Time: 1947
gelatin-silver print
13½ x 10½ inches
1981.80
Not illustrated

A clock found in a strange, partly-abandoned house on Bayou Lafourche. Its hands had stopped, untold years before. Birds had built a nest in the base of the clock, and when the birds had left, spiders went to work, weaving a gray and ghostly face in the cobwebs—the face, perhaps, of grim Time itself. CJL

The Interior Sun: 1946
gelatin-silver print
13½ x 10¼ inches
1981.81
Not illustrated

Afton Villa, near St. Francisville, La., was unique among the Louisiana plantations—it was a Gothic Revival house from 1849, but in recent years, has been tragically destroyed from fire. It had two staircases, each different, and here we see the 3-storied spiral one encased in one of the two turrets attached to the house. We look directly up its well—as it swirls aloft with almost unequaled grace—its lines as pure as the inner whorls in a sea shell. At top, a light hangs like a suspended sun—this was very probably the most perfect tight spiral staircase in Louisiana, until its destruction. CJL

Gods of the Mountain: 1954
gelatin-silver print
13⅞ x 10⅞ inches
1981.83
Not illustrated

A tremendous peak in the Garden of the Gods (Colorado) is alive with sculpture created by the enduring and mysterious magic of Time and Chance. At left center there is a massive Indian's head (in profile); directly above it (also in profile) is a large and singular fish head (aeons ago, there was an inland sea in this region); directly below, there are the blunt nose, and massive jaw, of a head whose eyes cannot be seen; directly to the right of the Indian's head is a tall figure with an elongated arm, and a hooded head. . .And there are other figures and semblances, too, but they must first be seen with the "Eye of the Subconscious"—rather than merely the physical eye. Enough has been revealed to indicate that this mountain summoned up its own "Spirit of Place" by recreating, in stone, some of the life forms involved in its own long existence; by projecting, in a neutral iconography, the intrinstic nature of this country. . .perhaps there is a creative spirit in the earth itself. CJL

The Portent in the Shadow: 1954
gelatin-silver print
13 x 10½ inches
1981.83
Illustrated on page 17

A traffic sign throws a shadow on an ancient Vieux Carre wall in New Orleans. But, looking closely, we discover in the shadow a one-eyed face with a helpless mouth, while the arrow points to nothingness. This image speaks to us, disquietly, of our confusion, of our loss of direction. It speaks to us in a secret language which exists everywhere, even in the most "inanimate" objects—for it is the language with which man impregnates all the objects around himself when defending himself against the inhumanity of things. CJL

Black Flames in the Sand
gelatin-silver print
10⅝ x 13⅞ inches
1981.84
Not illustrated

Made on the California seacoast, and showing rivulets of water running through the sand. However, when this image is inverted (which is why it was made)—space becomes reversed, and everything that was indented then becomes in relief, and fierce black flames seem to be coursing through the sand. This picture suggests the hidden, and magical, powers of the earth—and indicates how deceptive our physical vision can be. CJL

The Translucent Triangle: 1964
gelatin-silver print
13⅝ x 10⅝ inches
1981.85
Illustrated on page 16

This is the rear face of a solid memorial pyramid, containing a tomb, in a Milwaukee cemetery. But the flat surface now becomes non-solid, and non-flat—and we go into a mysterious inner space—which exists visually but not physically (that is, it exists only in this photograph)—and therefore, is not space that the eye could perceive when actually looking at the object. So both the magic of the camera and the mystery of space are involved in the creation of this picture. CJL

Flowers of the Night Land: 1958
gelatin-silver print
10¼ x 13⅛ inches
1981.86
Illustrated on page 14

Conveyed in this negative print is something of the feeling of the enormous and endless black plain of the night land, the land of the nocturnal mind. Only a spare leafless tree thrusts upward; while below are tight and secretive flowers—as tight and secretive as repressed thoughts. Naturalistically, this print derives from a vertical transparency of a clump of artificial flowers hanging on the wall of a New Orleans tomb. But in the "transcendence" which this print represents, every spatial relationship, as seen by the eye—as well as all the "normal" meanings of the objects—has been completely altered. CJL

Figure Floating on Its Own Reflection: 1957
gelatin-silver print
13½ x 10¾ inches
1981.87
Illustrated on page 17

A memorial to a man who was, apparently, a religious fanatic. The over-sized marble figure is so photographed that it seems to float on a strange liquid surface, while staring at us with all the force of obsession. Around, there is a feeling of a chapel of nightmare, with suggestions of an after-world. Again, an instance of the "unreality" of the "real". . . CJL

Born of the Earth (No. 2): 1952
gelatin-silver print
10¾ x 13¼ inches
1981.88
Not illustrated

On the balcony of this adobe house in New Mexico—born entirely of the earth—a mysterious figure arises—its form generated partly by Indian basketry, and, by a ferocious Totemic mask. Its tall isolation expresses something of the lonely and tragic destiny of Indian culture; something of the bitter fate of the people who gave their blood to this land, and whose strength came from the eternal and mysterious earth itself. . . CJL

The Improbable Dome: 1964
gelatin-silver print
13⅝ x 10½ inches
1981.89
Not illustrated

During the 1880s and '90s, Lake Geneva—one of the loveliest lakes in mid-America—was the summer resort for the Chicago millionaires. One of the most remarkable of all the great houses built on its shores was for Gordon Selfridge, at that time an associate of Marshall Field (later, to build the world-famous department store in London). The house is still owned by a wealthy Chicago family, and up to this time had not been photographed. On entering we are met with a truly magical sight: the living room has a huge painted ceiling (in green and gold) 3 floors up, and in this ceiling is set possibly the most lovely Tiffany glass dome in the U.S. Almost the whole interior of the house is treated in the Moorish Revival manner, and its colorful splendor seems as improbable as the Arabian Nights. CJL

Tree of Immensity: 1949
gelatin-silver print
13⅜ x 10⅝ inches
1981.90
Not illustrated

The Old Louisiana State Capitol goes back to 1849; but during the Civil War it was badly damaged. In the period 1880-82 the building was re-designed by the architect William A. Freret (its exterior being created in the Gothic Revival mode) while, within, was installed one of the most remarkable cast iron and glass domes left anywhere now from 19th century America. Created as though by a Piranesi of an Iron-age technology—a dramatic central column soars over 100 feet towards the apex of the dome. . . CJL

The Iron Flower: 1949
gelatin-silver print
13⅞ x 10⅞ inches
1981.91
Not illustrated

See *The Iron Shell: 1949*. The point at which the great central iron column unfolds into the ribs of the arches (the top and bottom of this print) then exfoliates into the magnificent cast-iron flower seen here, each panel curved, and cast in one piece, with its interstices open. Beyond the top of the "flower" is a skylight. Around, tier after tier of iron Gothic Revival arches, bolted together, rise upwards, being also a marvelous example of exposed structure long before the "modern" architects. The dome itself is composed of sheets of glass of many different colors. This is, then, an American equivalent, in a sense, of Coleridge's visonary dome of Kubla Khan. CJL

The Iron Shell: 1949
gelatin-silver print on paper
(drymounted on paperboard)
10¾ x 13½ inches
1981.92
Illustrated on page 15

And then, looking down from aloft in the dome, we can see the spiral staircase of cast iron. Its geometry is as pure as a nautilus shell, while the space between the first and second floors (which are covered with black and white marble squares) becomes strangely flattened. CJL

The Bat: 1940
gelatin-silver print
21 x 15⅝ inches
1981.93
Illustrated on front cover

In an imitation ruined abbey in a New Orleans cemetery—(even the cracks in the wall are faked!)—this image of hypocrisy appropriately appears. Batlike, hypocrisy flits everywhere, for it appears everywhere—in church, state, big business—its head cunningly concealed (as with those who turn their heads, hypocritically, from all that gives the lie to their own untruths). And while they preach peace and humanity, the people of hypocrisy lead us, actually, into confusion, war, and destruction.

CJL

SELECTED INDIVIDUAL EXHIBITIONS
1981: *Clarence John Laughlin,* Atlanta Gallery of Photography ∘ 1980: *The Third World of Photography,* Musee Nicephore Niepce, Chalon-sur-Saône, France ∘ 1978: *The Third World of Photography: The World Beyond Documentation and Purism,* Addison Gallery of American Art, Andover, Massachusetts ∘ 1973: *The Personal Eye,* Philadelphia Museum of Art ∘ 1940: Julien Levy Gallery, New York City, with Eugene Atget.

SELECTED GROUP EXHIBITIONS
1982: *Weston and Laughlin in Louisiana,* New Orleans Museum of Art ∘ 1978: *American Surrealism,* Rutgers University, Brunswick, New Jersey ∘ 1975: Museum of Modern Art, New York ∘ 1962: *Subjective Photography Show No. 2,* Otto Steinert Gallery, Cologne ∘ 1955: *Four Photographers: Atget, Stieglitz, Berenice Abbott and Laughlin,* Yale University Art Gallery, New Haven, Connecticut.

SELECTED MUSEUM COLLECTIONS
The Metropolitan Museum of Art, New York ∘ The Phillips Gallery, Washington, D.C. ∘ The Fogg Museum of Art, Harvard University, Cambridge, Massachusetts ∘ Philadelphia Museum of Art ∘ University of Louisville Photo Archives, Louisville, Kentucky ∘ Museum of Modern Art, New York.

Chuck Close
Born 1940, Monroe, Washington
Lives in New York City

Self-Portrait (3 parts lower half), 1980
polaroid
77 x 43¼ inches
76½ x 43½ inches
76 x 43½ inches
1981.162a, b, c
Illustrated on page 35

SELECTED INDIVIDUAL EXHIBITIONS
1980-1981: *Retrospective,* Walker Art Center, Minneapolis ∘ 1979: Georges Pompidou Centre, Paris ∘ 1979: The Pace Gallery, New York ∘ 1975: Baltimore Museum of Art, Baltimore ∘ 1973: Museum of Modern Art, New York.

SELECTED GROUP EXHIBITIONS
1981-1982: *Photographer as Printmaker,* Arts Council of Great Britain ∘ 1981-1982: *Instant Photography,* Stedelijk Museum, Amsterdam ∘ 1981: *Seven Photo-Realists,* Solomon R. Guggenheim Museum, New York ∘ 1977: *Representation of America,* The Metropolitan Museum of Art, New York, travelling show ∘ 1977: *Documenta 6,* Kassel, West Germany ∘ 1977: *Whitney Biennial,* Whitney Museum of American Art, New York ∘ 1976: *Three Decades of American Art,* Whitney Museum of American Art for Seibu Museum of Art, Tokyo ∘ 1975: *34th Biennial Exhibition of Contemporary Art,* Corcoran Gallery, Washington, D.C.

SELECTED MUSEUM AND PUBLIC COLLECTIONS
The Metropolitan Museum of Art, New York ∘ Museum of Contemporary Art, Chicago ∘ Museum of Modern Art, New York ∘ Whitney Museum of American Art, New York ∘ Philadelphia Museum of Art ∘ Hedenaagse Museum, Utrecht, Holland ∘ Portland Art Museum, Portland, Oregon.

Judy Dater
Born 1941, Hollywood, California
Lives in San Anselmo, California

Self-Portrait, Salt Flats, 1981
gelatin-silver print
18½ x 14½ inches
1981.170
Not illustrated

Self-Portrait on Deserted Road, 1982
gelatin-silver print
14¼ x 18⅜ inches
1982.274
Illustrated on page 29

SELECTED INDIVIDUAL EXHIBITIONS
1983: University of Oregon, Eugene, Oregon ∘ 1982: Baker Gallery, Kansas City, Kansas ∘ 1980: G. Ray Hopkins Gallery, Los Angeles ∘ 1979: Witkin Gallery, New York ∘ 1978: Grapestake Gallery, San Francisco ∘ 1975: Oakland Museum, Oakland, California.

SELECTED GROUP EXHIBITIONS
1982: *California Photographers,* Rhode Island School of Design, Providence ∘ 1978: *Mirrors and Windows: American Photography since 1960,* Museum of Modern Art, New York ∘ 1977: *Great West: Real Flash Ideals,* University of Colorado, Boulder ∘ 1974: *Private Realities,* Museum of Fine Arts, Boston ∘ 1973: *Judy Dater/Jack Welpott, Sisters,* International Museum of Photography, George Eastman House, Rochester, New York.

SELECTED MUSEUM AND PUBLIC COLLECTIONS
Center for Creative Photography, University of Arizona, Tuscon ∘ Art Institute of Chicago ∘ International Museum of Photography, George Eastman House, Rochester, New York ∘ The Museum of Modern Art, New York ∘ San Francisco Museum of Modern Art ∘ Los Angeles County Museum of Art.

Rita DeWitt

Born 1948, Covington, Kentucky
Lives in Hattiesburg, Mississippi

Q. Throughout the folds of eternity mind and flesh seek one another. A. Choose one: 1) True 2) False 3) Don't know, 1982
collage: xerox, pencil, crayon, and marshal oils
22½ x 30 inches
1983.19
Illustrated on page 22

SELECTED INDIVIDUAL EXHIBITIONS
1982: *Personal Images in Photo-Media,* The UAH Gallery of Art, University of Alabama-Huntsville, Alabama ◦ 1982: Photography Gallery 417, Prairie State College, Chicago ◦ 1982: *Cameracases,* University of Arkansas, Fayetteville ◦ 1982: Southern Light Gallery, Amarillo, Texas ◦ 1981: Meridian Museum of Art, Meridian, Mississippi ◦ 1980: The 4th Street Photo Gallery, New York.

SELECTED GROUP EXHIBITIONS
1982: *Photo/Flow,* University of Texas, Arlington ◦ 1982: *Photo-Collage,* Contemporary Arts Museum, Houston ◦ 1982: *The Modified Print,* Southeastern Graphics Invitational/1982: The Mint Museum of Art, Charlotte, North Carolina ◦ 1982: *New Photographics/82,* Central Washington University, Ellensburg, Washington ◦ 1982: *Joan Lyons/Rita DeWitt,* The Light Factory, Charlotte, North Carolina ◦ 1979: *Hot Shots: 25 Photographers,* Southeastern Center for Contemporary Art, Winston-Salem, North Carolina.

SELECTED MUSEUM AND PUBLIC COLLECTIONS
The Fogg Art Museum, Harvard University, Cambridge, Massachusetts ◦ University of Southern Mississippi, Department of Art, Hattiesburg, Mississippi ◦ Meridian Museum of Art, Meridian, Mississippi ◦ Georgia Power Company, Atlanta.

William Eggleston

Born 1939, Memphis
Lives in Memphis

Algiers, Louisiana
negative c.1974, print c.1976
type C color print
15 x 10⅛ inches
1982.10
Not illustrated

Outskirts of Morton, Mississippi, Halloween, 1971
image 1971, print 1982
dye transfer print (artist's proof from edition of 15)
11⅞ x 17¾ inches
1982.56
Not illustrated

Untitled (Freezer)
image ca. 1971-73, print 1980
dye transfer print (plate 6, 22/30, from "Troubled Waters Portfolio")
11½ x 17½ inches
1983.55
Illustrated on page 47

SELECTED INDIVIDUAL EXHIBITIONS
1982: Atlanta Gallery of Photography ◦ 1982: Lunn Gallery, Washington, D.C. ◦ 1977: Frumkin Gallery, Chicago ◦ 1977: Castelli Graphics, New York; Brooks Memorial Art Gallery, Memphis ◦ 1976: Museum of Modern Art, New York.

SELECTED GROUP EXHIBITIONS
1981: *The New Color,* International Center of Photography, New York ◦ 1979: *American Images: New Work by Twenty Contemporary Photographers,* Corcoran Gallery of Art, Washington, D.C. ◦ 1978: *The Quality of Presence,* Lunn Gallery, Washington, D.C. ◦ 1977: *Mirrors and Windows: American Photography Since 1960,* Museum of Modern Art, New York ◦ 1977: *William Eggleston/William Christenberry,* Morgan Gallery, Shawnee Mission, Kansas ◦ 1977: *The Contemporary South,* New Orleans Museum of Art.

SELECTED MUSEUM AND PUBLIC COLLECTIONS
San Francisco Museum of Modern Art ◦ The Art Institute of Chicago ◦ New Orleans Museum of Art ◦ The Museum of Modern Art, New York ◦ Dallas Museum of Fine Arts ◦ The Museum of Fine Arts, Houston.

Mario Giacomelli
Born 1925, Senigallia, Italy
Lives in Senigallia, Italy

Scanno (B-SC56), 1963
gelatin-silver print
11⅜ x 15½ inches
1981.155
Not illustrated

Paesaggio #20, 1970
gelatin-silver print
11⅞ x 13¾ inches
1981.156
Illustrated on page 32

SELECTED INDIVIDUAL EXHIBITIONS
1983: Robert Klein Gallery, Boston ◦ 1981: Rondaninni Gallery, Rome, Italy ◦ 1980: University of Parma, Italy ◦ 1980: Museum of Art, Rhode Island School of Design, Providence ◦ 1978: The Visual Studies Workshop, Rochester, New York ◦ 1977: Optica Gallery, Montreal, Canada.

SELECTED GROUP EXHIBITIONS
1982: California Museum of Photography, Riverside, California ◦ 1979: *Venice '79*, International Symposium and Exhibition of Photography, Venice, Italy ◦ 1979: *Venice Biennale*, Venice, Italy ◦ 1968: Centro D'Arte, Pescara, Italy ◦ 1966: Saletta Gallery, Florence, Italy.

SELECTED MUSEUM AND PUBLIC COLLECTIONS
Museum of Modern Art, New York ◦ Victoria and Albert Museum, London ◦ International Museum of Photography, George Eastman House, Rochester, New York ◦ Museum of Fine Arts, Boston.

Laura Gilpin
Born 1891, Colorado Springs
Died 1979, Santa Fe, New Mexico

Campo Santo, 1961
gelatin-silver print
9½ x 7¾ inches
1981.154
Illustrated on page 25

SELECTED INDIVIDUAL EXHIBITIONS
1974: *Laura Gilpin, Retrospective: 1910-1974*, Museum of New Mexico, Santa Fe ◦ 1974: Museum of New Mexico, Santa Fe ◦ 1973: Witkin Gallery, New York ◦ 1970: Oklahoma Art Center, Oklahoma City ◦ 1969: West Texas Museum, Lubbock, Texas.

SELECTED GROUP EXHIBITIONS
1979: *Recollection: Ten Women of Photography*, International Center of Photography, New York ◦ 1979: *Photography Rediscovered: American Photographs, 1900-1930*, Whitney Museum of American Art, New York ◦ 1977: *Photography, The Selected Image*, Edinboro State College, Edinboro, Pennsylvania ◦ 1975: *Women of Photography: An Historical Survey*, San Francisco Museum of Art ◦ 1953: *The West*, Colorado Springs Fine Art Center, Colorado Springs, Colorado.

SELECTED MUSEUM AND PUBLIC COLLECTIONS
The Amon Carter Museum, Fort Worth, Texas ◦ International Museum of Photography, George Eastman House, Rochester, New York ◦ Museum of Modern Art, New York ◦ New Orleans Museum of Art ◦ National Collection of Fine Arts, Washington, D.C. ◦ Library of Congress, Washington, D.C.

Jerry Gordon
Born 1949, Chicago
Lives in Chicago and New York

The Breakers Hotel, Palm Beach, Fla.
negative 1978, print 1979
cibachrome print, 3/15
17⅝ x 11½ inches
1983.30
Illustrated on page 39

SELECTED INDIVIDUAL EXHIBITIONS
1982: Photo Gallery, New York ∘ 1981: Southern Light Gallery, Amarillo, Texas ∘ 1980: University of Dayton, Dayton, Ohio ∘ 1980: Douglas Kenyon Gallery, Chicago ∘ 1978: Evanston Art Center, Evanston, Illinois.

SELECTED GROUP EXHIBITIONS
1981: PS1 Long Island, New York ∘ 1980: Light Gallery, New York ∘ 1980: Philadelphia Museum of Art ∘ 1980: The Museum School Gallery, Boston ∘ 1979: Vision Gallery, Boston ∘ 1979: Alfred University, New York ∘ 1976: ARC Gallery, Chicago.

SELECTED MUSEUM AND PUBLIC COLLECTIONS
California Museum of Photography, Riverside, California ∘ Corcoran Gallery, Washington, D.C. ∘ Illinois Institute of Technology, Chicago, Illinois ∘ Library of Congress, Washington, D.C.

Emmet Gowin
Born 1941, Danville, Virginia
Lives in Newton, Pennsylvania

Family, Danville, Va.
negative 1969, printed 1976
gelatin-silver print on paper
5¼ x 6¾ inches
1981.157
Illustrated on page 28

SELECTED INDIVIDUAL EXHIBITIONS
1983: *Retrospective,* Corcoran Gallery, Washington, D.C. ∘ 1983: Nexus Gallery, Atlanta ∘ 1979: Light Gallery, New York ∘ 1978: Photographer's Gallery and Workshop, Sidney, Australia ∘ 1977: Susan Spiritus Gallery, Newport Beach, California ∘ 1973: Museum of Modern Art (two-man show with Robert Adams), New York ∘ 1973: Cocoran Gallery, Washington, D.C.

SELECTED GROUP EXHIBITIONS
1983: *Harry Callahan and his Students: A Study in Influences,* Georgia State University, Atlanta ∘ 1978: *Mirrors and Windows: American Photography since 1960,* Museum of Modern Art, New York ∘ 1975: *Celebrations,* MIT, Cambridge, Massachusetts ∘ 1974: *Private Realities,* Museum of Fine Arts, Boston ∘ 1974: *Photography in America,* Whitney Museum of American Art, New York ∘ 1971: *Photographs by Robert Adams and Emmet Gowin,* Museum of Modern Art, New York.

SELECTED MUSEUM AND PUBLIC COLLECTIONS
Museum of Modern Art, New York ∘ The Fogg Art Museum, Harvard University, Cambridge, Massachusetts ∘ International Museum of Photography, George Eastman House, Rochester, New York ∘ New Orleans Museum of Fine Arts ∘ National Gallery of Canada, Ottawa ∘ Yale University, New Haven, Connecticut.

Richard Scott Hill
Born 1942, Fort Myers, Florida
Lives in Atlanta

Lyn–From the Rembrandt Mask Series, 1982
gelatin-silver print, 2/10
18½ x 14 inches
1983.26
Illustrated on page 44

SELECTED INDIVIDUAL EXHIBITIONS
1983: Fay Gold Gallery, Atlanta ∘ 1977: Nexus Gallery, Atlanta.

SELECTED GROUP EXHIBITIONS
1983: *New Discoveries,* Robert Samuel Gallery, New York ∘ 1983: *Atlanta Now–Focus on Photography,* Robert Freidus Gallery, New York ∘ 1975: *Artists Biennial,* New Orleans Museum of Art ∘ 1975: Museum of Contemporary Art, Olinda, Recife, Brazil ∘ 1971,1973,1974: *Artists in Georgia,* High Museum of Art, Atlanta ∘ 1972: Pushkin Museum, Moscow, Russia.

SELECTED MUSEUM AND PUBLIC COLLECTIONS
Augusta Richmond County Museum, Augusta, Georgia ∘ Atlanta Civic Center, Atlanta ∘ High Museum of Art, Atlanta ∘ Pushkin Museum, Moscow, Russia.

Kenneth Josephson
Born 1932, Detroit, Michigan
Lives in Chicago

Chicago, 1969
photo-collage, gelatin-silver print with 4 color postcard sections attached, 6/40
4 x 6 inches
1983.49
Illustrated on page 31

SELECTED INDIVIDUAL EXHIBITIONS
1981: Young Hoffman Gallery, Chicago ∘ 1979: Photographers Gallery, London ∘ 1978: Fotoforum, Kassel, Federal Republic of Germany ∘ 1976: Camera Works Gallery, Los Angeles ∘ 1971: Visual Studies Workshop, Rochester, New York ∘ 1971: The Art Institute of Chicago.

SELECTED GROUP EXHIBITIONS
1983: *Harry Callahan and his Students: A Study in Influences*, Georgia State University, Atlanta ∘ 1981: *Crane, Jachna, Josephson, Larson, Metzker/An Exhibition of Photographers*, Fine Arts Center Gallery, University of Arkansas, Fayetteville ∘ 1980: *Invented Images*, USCB Art Museum, University of Southern California, Santa Barbara ∘ 1979: *American Photographs of the Seventies*, Art Institute of Chicago ∘ 1978: *Mirrors and Windows: American Photography Since 1960*, Museum of Modern Art, New York ∘ 1977: *The Great West, Real/Ideal*, University of Colorado, Boulder.

SELECTED MUSEUM AND PUBLIC COLLECTIONS
Art Institute of Chicago ∘ Center for Creative Photography, University of Arizona, Tuscon ∘ International Museum of Photography, George Eastman House, Rochester, New York ∘ John Simon Guggenheim Memorial Foundation, New York ∘ The Metropolitan Museum of Art, New York.

Leah Jaynes Karp
Born 1940, Pontiac, Illinois
Lives in Philadelphia

Altanta Children's Notebook #1-12
mixed media
dimensions varied
1983.62.1-12
#5 illustrated on page 46

SELECTED INDIVIDUAL EXHIBITIONS
1979: Pittsburgh Filmmakers, Pittsburgh ∘ 1979: University Art Gallery, University of South Dakota, Vermillion, South Dakota.

SELECTED GROUP EXHIBITIONS
1983: *Handmade Cameras: Contemporary Images*, Tyler School of Art, Temple University, Philadelphia ∘ 1981: Black and Hispanic Arts Festival, Balch Institute, Philadelphia ∘ 1980: *Faculty Art Show*, Moore College of Art, Philadelphia ∘ 1979: *New Art Group Show*, Nexus Gallery, Philadelphia ∘ 1977: *Images of Women*, Portland Museum of Art, Portland, Maine.

SELECTED MUSEUM AND PUBLIC COLLECTIONS
Portland Museum of Art, Portland, Maine ∘ Bellevue Art Museum, Bellevue, Washington.

Josef Koudelka
Born 1938, Boscovice, Czechoslovakia
Lives in Paris

Bardejov, 1967
gelatin-silver print
14¼ x 9¼ inches
1982.55
Not illustrated

Velka Lomnica, 1963
print 1983
9⅛ x 14¼ inches
1983.52
Illustrated on page 45

SELECTED INDIVIDUAL EXHIBITIONS
1981: The Carpenter Center for Visual Arts, Harvard University, Cambridge, Massachusetts ∘ 1980: Photography Gallery, Philadelphia ∘ 1979: Fototeca Gallery, Caracas, Venezuela ∘ 1978: The Stedelijk Museum, Amsterdam ∘ 1976: The Art Institute of Chicago ∘ 1975: Carlton Gallery, New York ∘ 1968: *An Exhibition of Theater Photography*, Theater Za Branou, Prague.

SELECTED MUSEUM AND PUBLIC COLLECTIONS
Museum of Modern Art, New York ∘ Philadelphia Museum of Art ∘ The Art Institute of Chicago.

William G. Larson
Born 1942, North Tonawonda, New York
Lives in Wyncote, Pennsylvania

Untitled, 1979-80
polaroid print
24⅛ x 20½ inches
1983.25
Illustrated on page 30

SELECTED INDIVIDUAL EXHIBITIONS
1983: International Museum of Photography, George Eastman House, Rochester, New York ∘ 1983: Center for Creative Photography, University of Arizona, Tuscon ∘ 1981: Light Gallery, New York ∘ 1980: Los Angeles Institute of Contemporary Art ∘ 1978: Camera Work Gallery, San Francisco ∘ 1978: Art Institute of Chicago.

SELECTED GROUP EXHIBITIONS
1981: *The Still Life,* Museum of Modern Art, New York ∘ 1981: *Whitney Biennial,* Whitney Museum of American Art, New York ∘ 1980: *American Color Photography,* Galerie Rudolf Kitchen, Cologne, Germany ∘ 1979: *Electroworks,* International Museum of Photography, George Eastman House, Rochester, New York ∘ 1977: *Locations in Time,* International Museum of Photography, George Eastman House, Rochester, New York ∘ 1972: *The Expanded Photograph,* Philadelphia Museum of Art.

SELECTED MUSEUM AND PUBLIC COLLECTIONS
The Center for Creative Photography, University of Arizona, Tuscon ∘ Galleries of the Claremont Colleges, Claremont, California ∘ New Orleans Museum of Art ∘ Museum of Modern Art, New York ∘ Visual Studies Workshop, Rochester, New York ∘ Philadelphia Museum of Art.

Stephen Livick
Born 1945, England
Lives in Toronto, Ontario

Untitled, 1981
color separated bichromate gum print on paper, hand-colored, 4/10
27 x 27⅛ inches
1982.59
Illustrated on page 23

SELECTED INDIVIDUAL EXHIBITIONS
1978: Baltimore Museum of Art, Baltimore ∘ 1978: Platinum Prints, David Mirvish Gallery, Toronto ∘ 1976: Photography Gallery, Bowmanville, Ontario ∘ 1975: International Museum of Photography, George Eastman House, Rochester, New York ∘ 1973: London Public Art Gallery, London ∘ 1972: Centaur Gallery, Montreal.

SELECTED GROUP EXHIBITIONS
1978: *Photographic Landscapes:* International Museum of Photography, George Eastman House, Rochester, New York ∘ 1977: National Film Board of Canada, The Photo Gallery, Ottawa ∘ 1977: *New Acquisitions,* National Gallery of Canada, Ottawa ∘ 1976: Robert Schoelkopf Gallery, New York ∘ 1976: *Exposure,* Art Gallery of Ontario, Toronto ∘ 1975: National Art Gallery, Ottawa.

SELECTED MUSEUM AND PUBLIC COLLECTIONS
Museum of Modern Art, New York ∘ George Eastman House, Rochester, New York ∘ The Fogg Art Museum, Harvard University, Cambridge, Massachusetts ∘ Art Bank, Ottawa ∘ Kunstmuseum, Basel, Switzerland ∘ National Film Board of Canada ∘ National Gallery of Canada, Ottawa.

Ralph Eugene Meatyard
Born 1925, Normal, Illinois
Died 1972, Lexington, Kentucky

Untitled, 1961
gelatin-silver print
6⅛ x 5¼ inches
1983.29
Illustrated on page 24

SELECTED INDIVIDUAL EXHIBITIONS
1971: Art Institute of Chicago ∘ 1971: Massachusetts Institute of Technology, Cambridge ∘ 1970: Ohio University, Athens, Ohio ∘ 1970: Center for Photographic Studies, Lexington, Kentucky ∘ 1967: J. B. Speed Museum, Lexington, Kentucky ∘ 1962: Carl Siembab Gallery, Boston.

SELECTED GROUP EXHIBITIONS
1972: *The Multiple Image,* Creative Photography Gallery, MIT, Cambridge, Massachusetts ∘ 1971: *Photographs from the Coke Collection,* Everson Museum of Art, Syracuse, New York ∘ 1969-1970: *The Camera and the Human Facade,* Smithsonian Institution, Washington, D.C. ∘ 1969: *Light,* Massachusetts Institute of Technology, Cambridge, Massachusetts ∘ 1967: *Photography of the Twentieth Century,* National Gallery of Canada, Ottawa ∘ 1959: *Sense of Abstraction,* Museum of Modern Art, New York.

SELECTED MUSEUM AND PUBLIC COLLECTIONS
Art Institute of Chicago ∘ Museum of Modern Art, New York ∘ New Orleans Museum of Art ∘ Philadelphia Museum of Art ∘ International Museum of Photography, George Eastman House, Rochester, New York ∘ Massachusetts Institute of Technology, Cambridge.

Ray K. Metzker
Born 1931, Milwaukee, Wisconsin
Lives in Philadelphia

Untitled from "Pictus Interruptus," 1977
gelatin-silver print
11⅝ x 17⅛ inches
1981.158
Illustrated on page 20

SELECTED INDIVIDUAL EXHIBITIONS
1979: *"Venezia '79,"* La Fotographia, Venice, Italy ∘ 1976: The Picture Gallery, Zurich, Switzerland ∘ 1974: Philadelphia Print Club ∘ 1971: University of New Mexico, Albequerque ∘ 1970: Wisconsin Heritage, Milwaukee Art Center, Milwaukee ∘ 1967: Museum of Modern Art, New York.

SELECTED GROUP EXHIBITIONS
1983: *Harry Callahan and His Students: A Study in Influences,* Georgia State University, Atlanta ∘ 1981: *Crane, Jachna, Josephson, Carson, Metzker/An Exhibition of Photographs,* Fine Arts Center Gallery, University of Arkansas, Fayetteville ∘ 1978: *Mirrors and Windows: American Photography Since 1960,* Museum of Modern Art, New York ∘ 1977: *The Photographer and the City,* Museum of Contemporary Art, Chicago ∘ 1973: *Landscape/Cityscape,* Metropolitan Museum of Art, New York ∘ 1970: *New Photography U.S.A.,* Museum of Modern Art, New York.

SELECTED MUSEUM AND PUBLIC COLLECTIONS
Art Institute of Chicago ∘ International Museum of Photography, George Eastman House, Rochester, New York ∘ The Metropolitan Museum of Art, New York ∘ Museum of Modern Art, New York ∘ Museum of Fine Arts, Houston ∘ Philadelphia Museum of Art.

Duane Michals
Born 1932, McKeesport, Pennsylvania
Lives in New York City

Self-Portrait 1979 with Pablo Picasso 1909
oil on gelatin-silver print
11 x 13⅞ inches
1981.159
Illustrated on page 19

A Failed Attempt to Photograph Reality, 1975
ink on photographic paper 6/25
8 x 9-15/16 inches
1983.10
Not illustrated

SELECTED INDIVIDUAL EXHIBITIONS
1982: La Remise du Parc, Paris ∘ 1981: Philadelphia College of Art ∘ 1980: Sidney Janis Gallery, New York ∘ 1976: Contemporary Arts Center, Cincinnati, Ohio ∘ 1972: San Francisco Art Institute ∘ 1970: Museum of Modern Art, New York.

SELECTED GROUP EXHIBITIONS
1982: *In Sequence,* Museum of Fine Arts, Houston ∘ 1980: *First Person Singular: Recent Self-Portraiture,* Pratt Institute, New York ∘ 1978: *Art About Art,* Whitney Museum of American Art, New York ∘ 1977: *American Narrative Art/Story Art,* Contemporary Arts Museum, Houston ∘ 1976: *Real, Unreal, Surreal,* San Diego State University, San Diego ∘ 1974: *Photography in America,* Whitney Museum of American Art, New York.

SELECTED MUSEUM AND PUBLIC COLLECTIONS
Art Institute of Chicago ∘ International Museum of Photography, George Eastman House, Rochester, New York ∘ Museum of Modern Art, New York ∘ Museum of Fine Arts, Boston ∘ New Orleans Museum of Art ∘ National Gallery of Canada, Ottawa.

Lisette Model
Born 1906, Vienna, Austria
Died 1983, New York City

New York, ca. 1951
gelatin-silver print
13½ x 10½ inches
1982.54
Illustrated on page 33

SELECTED INDIVIDUAL EXHIBITIONS
1979: *Lisette Model: Photographs,* Vision Gallery, Boston ∘ 1977: *The Photographs of Lisette Model,* Bucks County Community College, Newtown, Pennsylvania ∘ 1976: *Lisette Model Photographs,* Sander Gallery, Washington, D.C. ∘ 1974: *Photographs by Lisette Model,* Focus Gallery, San Francisco ∘ 1949: *Leading Photographers: Lisette Model,* Museum of Modern Art, New York ∘ 1943: *Photographs by Lisette Model,* The Chicago Art Institute, Chicago.

SELECTED GROUP EXHIBITIONS
1978: *The Quality of Presence,* Lunn Gallery, Washington, D.C. ∘ 1979: *Three Woman Show: Diane Arbus, Lisette Model, Rosalind Solomon,* Galerie Zabriskie, Paris ∘ 1975: *Women of Photography: An Historical Survey,* San Francisco Museum of Modern Art ∘ 1972: *Brodovitch and His Influence,* Philadelphia College of Art ∘ 1955: *The Family of Man,* Museum of Modern Art, New York ∘ 1948: *In and Out of Focus: A Survey of Today's Photography,* Museum of Modern Art, New York.

SELECTED MUSEUM AND PUBLIC COLLECTIONS
The Center for Creative Photography, University of Arizona, Tuscon ∘ New Orleans Museum of Art ∘ The Metropolitan Museum of Art, New York ∘ Museum of Modern Art, New York ∘ International Museum of Photography, George Eastman House, Rochester, New York ∘ The Museum of Fine Arts, Houston.

Lucas Samaras
Born 1936, Kastoria, Macedonia, Greece
Lives in New York City

Photo-Transformation, November 12, 1973
SX70 polaroid print
3 x 3⅛ inches
1983.24
Illustrated on page 34

SELECTED INDIVIDUAL EXHIBITIONS
1978: *Reconstructions and Photo-Transformations*, Akron Art Institute, Ohio ∘ 1977: *Photo-Transformations*, Walker Art Center, Minneapolis ∘ 1976: *Modern Art Pavilion*, Seattle Art Museum ∘ 1975: *Photo-Transformation*, Pace Gallery, New York ∘ 1970: Museum of Modern Art, New York ∘ 1972: *Retrospective*, Whitney Museum of American Art, New York.

SELECTED GROUP EXHIBITIONS
1978: *Mirrors and Windows: American Photography since 1960*, Museum of Modern Art, New York ∘ 1975: *Body Works*, Museum of Contemporary Art, Chicago ∘ 1973: *By SX-70*, Light Gallery, New York ∘ 1972: *Documenta*, Kassel, Germany ∘ 1968: *Dada, Surrealism and their Heritage*, Museum of Modern Art, New York ∘ 1968: *The Obsessive Image*, The Institute of Contemporary Art, London.

SELECTED MUSEUM AND PUBLIC COLLECTIONS
Museum of Modern Art, New York ∘ The Metropolitan Museum of Art, New York ∘ Solomon R. Guggenheim Museum of Art, New York ∘ Los Angeles County Museum of Art ∘ Hirshorn Museum and Sculpture Garden, Washington, D.C. ∘ Art Institute of Chicago.

Cindy Sherman
Born 1954, Glen Ridge, New Jersey
Lives in New York City

Untitled Film Still (Mirrored Bar-Phillips), 1979
gelatin-silver print
24¼ x 35⅞ inches
1981.160
Illustrated on page 36

SELECTED INDIVIDUAL EXHIBITIONS
1981: Metro Pictures, New York ∘ 1980: Contemporary Arts Museum, Houston ∘ 1980: The Kitchen Center, New York ∘ 1979: Hallwalls, Buffalo, New York ∘ 1977: Visual Studies Workshop, Rochester, New York ∘ 1976: Hallwalls, Buffalo, New York.

SELECTED GROUP EXHIBITIONS
1981: *On Location*, Texas Gallery, Houston ∘ 1980: *Likely Stories*, Castelli Graphics, New York ∘ 1980: *Remembrances for Tomorrow*, New 57 Gallery, Edinburgh, Scotland ∘ 1979: *Re-figuration*, Max Protetch Gallery, New York ∘ 1978: *Four Artists*, Artists Space, New York ∘ 1977: Albright-Knox Gallery, Buffalo, New York.

SELECTED MUSEUM AND PUBLIC COLLECTIONS
Dallas Museum of Fine Arts ∘ Museum of Modern Art, New York ∘ Tate Gallery, London ∘ Stedelijk, Amsterdam ∘ Centre George Pompidou, Paris ∘ Australian National Gallery, Canberra.

Laurel Simmons
Born 1949, Long Island, New York
Lives in New York City

Calumny: Detail Truth, 1981
cibachrome print
13⅜ x 19¾ inches
1983.31
Illustrated on page 38

SELECTED INDIVIDUAL EXHIBITIONS
1981: Diane Brown Gallery, Washington, D.C. ∘ 1981: Metro Pictures, New York ∘ 1979: Artists Space, New York ∘ 1979: P.S.1, Institute for Art and Urban Resources, Long Island City ∘ 1979: University of Rhode Island, Kingston.

SELECTED GROUP EXHIBITIONS
1981: Texas Gallery, Houston ∘ 1981: *Gender*, Group Materials, New York ∘ 1981: *Fabricated to be Photographed*, Wright State University, Dayton, Ohio ∘ 1980: *Remembrances for Tomorrow*, New 57 Gallery, Edinburgh, Scotland ∘ 1980: *Presences: The Figure and Man-Made Environments*, Freedman Gallery, Albright College, Reading, Pennsylvania ∘ 1980: *Invented Images*, University of California, Santa Barbara, Art Museum ∘ 1979: *Re-Figurations*, Max Protetch Gallery, New York.

SELECTED MUSEUM AND PUBLIC COLLECTIONS
Albright-Knox Gallery, Buffalo, New York ∘ The Fogg Art Museum, Harvard University, Cambridge, Massachusetts ∘ Museum of Fine Arts, Houston ∘ Allen Memorial Art Museum, Oberlin College, Oberlin, Ohio.

W. Eugene Smith
Born 1918, Wichita, Kansas
Died 1978, Tuscon, Arizona

Loft Inside (self-portrait) Texas, ca. 1963
gelatin-silver print
6⅝ x 9⅛ inches
1981.99
Illustrated on page 18

SELECTED INDIVIDUAL EXHIBITIONS
1979: *Life: The First Decade 1936-1945*, Grey Art Gallery and Study Center, New York University, New York ∘ 1978: *Photographs by W. Eugene Smith*, Victoria & Albert Museum, London, travelling exhibit ∘ 1976: Witkin Gallery, New York ∘ 1970: *Let Truth be the Prejudice*, Jewish Museum, New York ∘ 1966: *W. Eugene Smith*, George Eastman House, Rochester, New York ∘ 1958: *W. Eugene Smith*, Limelight Gallery, New York.

SELECTED GROUP EXHIBITIONS
1972: *Images of Concern*, Bienville Gallery, New Orleans ∘ 1970: *Multiple Exposure*, Philadelphia Museum of Art ∘ 1965: *The Photo Essay*, Museum of Modern Art, New York ∘ 1961: *Twentieth Century American Art: Painting, Drawing, Sculpture, Photography*, Kalamazoo Art Center, Kalamazoo, Michigan ∘ 1955: *The Family of Man*, Museum of Modern Art, New York ∘ 1952: *Diogenes with A Camera*, Museum of Modern Art, New York.

SELECTED MUSEUM AND PUBLIC COLLECTIONS
Museum of Modern Art, New York ∘ International Museum of Photography, George Eastman House, Rochester, New York ∘ The Fogg Art Museum, Harvard University, Cambridge, Massachusetts ∘ Art Institute of Chicago ∘ Menil Foundation, Houston ∘ New Orleans Museum of Art ∘ Philadelphia Museum of Art.

Virginia Warren Smith
Born 1947, Atlanta
Lives in Atlanta

Shrine to the Elephant Norma Jean, 1981
print 1982
gelatin-silver print, hand-colored with oils
11⅞ x 17⅜ inches
1982.60
Not illustrated

Body as Body, 1982
gelatin-silver print, hand-colored with oils
17½ x 11⅞ inches
1983.28
Not illustrated

Missing: One Electric Chair, 1982
gelatin-silver print, hand-colored with oils
8¾ x 12¾ inches
Gift of the artist for the Lucinda W. Bunnen Collection
1983.54
Illustrated on page 26

SELECTED INDIVIDUAL EXHIBITIONS
1982: *Recent Photographs*, Atlanta Gallery of Photography ∘ 1981: *Scoring in Heaven*, Chastain Art Center, Atlanta, with Lucinda Bunnen ∘ 1980: *Recent Photographs*, Columbia Museums of Art and Science, Columbia, South Carolina.

SELECTED GROUP EXHIBITIONS
1983: *New Photographics/83*, Central Washington State University, Ellensberg ∘ 1982: *The Importance of the Inter-Relationship Between Man and Animal*, The Photography Gallery, La Jolla, California ∘ 1982: *Artists in Georgia/82*, Lamar Dodd Art Center, LaGrange, Georgia ∘ 1979: *Hand-Colored Photographs*, Nexus Gallery, Atlanta ∘ 1978: *Southeastern Photography Competition*, Greenville County Museum of Art, Greenville, South Carolina ∘ 1977: *Southeastern Invitational Exhibition*, Southeastern Center for the Contemporary Arts, Winston-Salem, North Carolina

SELECTED MUSEUM AND PUBLIC COLLECTIONS
High Museum of Art, Atlanta ∘ Columbia Museums of Art and Science, Columbia, South Carolina.

Joel Sternfeld
Born 1944, New York City
Lives in New York City

Exhausted Renegade Elephant, Woodburn, Washington, June 1979
color dye transfer print, 4/50
13½ x 17⅛ inches
1983.53
Illustrated on page 42

SELECTED INDIVIDUAL EXHIBITIONS
1983: Photography Gallery, La Jolla, California ∘ 1982: Grapestake Gallery, San Francisco ∘ 1982: Brent Sikkema Gallery, Boston ∘ 1981: Daniel Wolf Gallery, Boston ∘ 1976: People House Galleries, Pennsylvania Academy of Fine Arts, Philadelphia.

SELECTED GROUP EXHIBITIONS
1981: *Color Landscape Photographs,* Creative Photography Galleries, MIT, Cambridge, Massachusetts ∘ 1981: *The New Color,* Everson Museum of Art, Syracuse, New York ∘ 1981: *Color Photography: New Images,* Mandeville Art Gallery, University of California at San Diego, La Jolla, California ∘ 1980: *Creative Artist's Public Service Photography Exhibition,* New York State University ∘ 1979: *Photographie Im Alltaglich Amerika,* Zurich, Switzerland ∘ 1979: *One of a Kind,* Polaroid Corporation, Cambridge, Massachusetts.

SELECTED MUSEUM AND PUBLIC COLLECTIONS
Museum of Modern Art, New York ∘ San Francisco Museum of Modern Art ∘ Houston Museum of Fine Arts ∘ Minneapolis Art Institute.

Robert B. Stewart
Born 1945, Richland, Washington
Lives in Atlanta

Self-Portrait, Santa Fe, 1978
hand typeset and printed paper
15½ x 20 inches
1983.51
Not illustrated

Self-Portrait, Montclair, N.J., 1982
hand typeset and printed paper
15½ x 20 inches
1983.50
Illustrated on page 41

SELECTED INDIVIDUAL EXHIBITIONS
1982: *Recent Work,* Cheatham Gallery, Thomson, Georgia ∘ 1978: *Photographs,* Northlight Gallery, Arizona State University, Tempe, Arizona.

SELECTED GROUP EXHIBITIONS
1982: *Distinguished Alumni,* Kemper Gallery, Kansas City Art Institute, Kansas City ∘ 1978: *The Instant Image,* Camerawork Gallery, San Francisco ∘ 1978: *Xerox/Xerox/Xerox,* University of Colorado, Boulder ∘ 1978: *Polaroid Collaboratory,* Open Space Gallery, Victoria, British Columbia.

Evon Streetman
Born 1932, Fort Meade, Florida
Lives in Gainesville, Florida

Love Before Breakfast, 1981
collage: airbrush with acrylic paint, pencil, colored pencil, photograph, thumbtacks, on masonite board primed with flat white enamel paint
35½ x 27½ inches
1983.18
Illustrated on page 43

SELECTED INDIVIDUAL EXHIBITIONS
1981: Deland Museum of Fine Arts, Florida ∘ 1978: Southeastern Center for the Contemporary Arts, Winston-Salem, North Carolina ∘ 1978: Daytona Beach Junior College, Daytona Beach, Florida ∘ 1978: *Facts and Fantasies,* University of Florida, Gainesville ∘ 1974: Duke University, Durham, North Carolina ∘ 1966: University of Georgia, Athens, Georgia.

SELECTED GROUP EXHIBITIONS
1982: *National Women in Art,* Edison Community College, Fort Myers, Florida ∘ 1982: *New Women, New Work,* Light Gallery, New York ∘ 1982: *Subtle Visions,* Griffith Gallery, Coral Gables, Florida ∘ 1980: *Vis a Vis,* The Art Institute of Boston ∘ 1979: *Eleven Southern Photographers,* Montgomery Museum of Fine Arts, Montgomery, Alabama ∘ 1978: *I Shall Save One Land Unvisited,* Corcoran Gallery, Washington, D.C.

SELECTED MUSEUM AND PUBLIC COLLECTIONS
Mint Museum, Charlotte, North Carolina ∘ Museum of Modern Art, New York ∘ International Museum of Photography, George Eastman House, Rochester, New York ∘ Jacksonville Art Museum, Jacksonville, Florida ∘ Museum of Fine Arts, Saint Petersburg, Florida ∘ College of Fine Arts/Galleries Program, University of Southern Florida, Tampa.

Martin Stupich
Born 1949, Milwaukee, Wisconsin
Lives in Reno, Nevada

Shield Operator, MARTA North Line Construction Below Peachtree Street, Between Peachtree Center and Five Points Station, Atlanta, Georgia
negative 1978, print 1981
gelatin-silver print on paper
9⅛ x 13¼ inches
1981.163
Not illustrated

Peachtree Center MARTA Station Under Construction
negative 1979, print 1981
gelatin-silver print
9⅛ x 13⅜ inches
1981.164
Not illustrated

Carnegie Library Demolition, Atlanta, Georgia, September
negative 1977, print 1981
gelatin-silver print
10 x 12½ inches
1981.165
Illustrated on page 40

Empty Parking Lot, Partly Demolished Buildings, Atlanta, Georgia
negative 1980, print 1981
gelatin-silver print
9⅛ x 13¼ inches
1981.166
Not illustrated

Five Points Station Site, MARTA Construction, November 1977, Atlanta, Georgia
negative 1977, print 1981
gelatin-silver print
10½ x 13⅛ inches
1981.167
Not illustrated

Demolition on Site of World Congress Center, With 101 Marietta Office Tower in Background, Atlanta, Georgia
negative 1977, print 1981
gelatin-silver print
10⅛ x 12½ inches
1981.168
Not illustrated

Half of Building, Parking Lot, Skyline, Atlanta, Georgia
negative 1979, print 1981
gelatin-silver print
9⅛ x 13⅛ inches
1981.169
Not illustrated

SELECTED INDIVIDUAL EXHIBITIONS
1982: Nevada Governors, Carson City, Nevada ∘ 1980: New Orleans Contemporary Arts Center ∘ 1979: North Virginia Community College, Sterling, Virginia ∘ 1978 and 1981: Nexus Gallery, Atlanta ∘ 1978: Atlanta Historical Society, Atlanta ∘ 1976: Princeton University.

SELECTED GROUP EXHIBITIONS
1983: Pacific University Gallery, Seattle, Washington ∘ 1983: *The World is Flat and Framed,* Reno, Nevada ∘ 1982: Middendorf Lane Gallery, Washington, D.C. ∘ 1980: Nexus Gallery, Atlanta ∘ 1977: Rizzoli Gallery, Atlanta ∘ 1975: Georgia State University, Atlanta.

SELECTED MUSEUM AND PUBLIC COLLECTIONS
National Museum of American Art, Smithsonian Institution, Washington, D.C. ∘ Atlanta Historical Society ∘ Georgia Power Company, Atlanta ∘ High Museum of Art, Atlanta ∘ National Archives, Washington, D.C. ∘ Library of Congress, Washington, D.C.

Elizabeth Turk

Born 1945, Fort Riley, Kansas
Lives in Atlanta

Self-Portrait, 1979 (5 photographs)
gelatin-silver prints
Each 11⅞ x 17⅝ inches
1981.161a, not illustrated
1981.161b, not illustrated
1981.161c, illustrated on page 21
1981.161d, not illustrated
1981.161e, not illustrated

SELECTED INDIVIDUAL EXHIBITIONS
1981: Two-Person show with Bill Burke, Nexus Gallery, Atlanta ◦ 1977: Two-Person show with Robert Stewart, Nexus Gallery, Atlanta ◦ 1976: Two-Person show with Sandy Noyes, Nexus Gallery, Atlanta.

SELECTED GROUP EXHIBITIONS
1982: Atlanta Photographers, Nexus Gallery, Atlanta ◦ 1982: Middendorf Lane Gallery, Washington, D.C. ◦ 1980: *The Never Fail Image*, The Museum School Gallery, Boston Museum of Art, Boston ◦ 1979: *Young Photographers*, The Atlanta Gallery of Photography, Atlanta ◦ 1977: *Women See Men*, MIT, Cambridge, Massachusetts ◦ 1976: Doculanta Exhibition, Peachtree Center, Atlanta.

PUBLIC COLLECTIONS
The City of Atlanta, Doculanta ◦ Georgia Power Company, Atlanta.

Arthur Tress

Born 1940, Brooklyn, New York
Lives in New York City

Charlotte Olds, Freeville, NY
negative 1976, print 1982
gelatin-silver print, 1/25
15¼ x 14⅞ inches
1982.57
Illustrated on page 37

Girl Collecting Goldfish, Chateau Breteuil, France
negative 1976, print 1982
gelatin-silver print
15¾ x 15½ inches
1982.58
Not illustrated

SELECTED INDIVIDUAL EXHIBITIONS
1981: Galerie Agathe, Gaillard, Paris ◦ 1980: *Arthur Tress: A Twelve Year Survey*, Robert Samuel Gallery, New York ◦ 1975: *Shadow*, Neikrug Gallery, New York ◦ 1973: *Vision Seekers*, SOHO Gallery, New York ◦ 1972: *The Dream Collector*, Raffi Photo Gallery, New York ◦ 1970: *Open Space in the Inner City*, Sierra Club Gallery, New York.

SELECTED GROUP EXHIBITIONS
1981: *The Nude*, MIT, Cambridge, Massachusetts ◦ 1979: *Photographic Surrealism*, New Gallery of Contemporary Art, Cleveland, Ohio ◦ 1979: *Attitudes: Photography in the 1970's*, Santa Barbara Museum of Art ◦ 1978: *Self-Portrait*, Friends of Photography, Carmel, California ◦ 1969: *Vision and Expression*, International Museum of Photography, George Eastman House, Rochester, New York.

SELECTED MUSEUM AND PUBLIC COLLECTIONS
Museum of Modern Art, New York ◦ The Metropolitan Museum of Art, New York ◦ International Museum of Photography, George Eastman House, Rochester, New York ◦ Centre George Pompidou, Paris ◦ Stedelijk Museum, Amsterdam ◦ Columbia College, Chicago.

William Wegman

Born 1942, Holyoke, Massachusetts
Lives in New York City

Spring Maples, 1981
SX70 polaroid
24⅛ x 20⅝ inches
1983.27
Illustrated on page 27

SELECTED INDIVIDUAL EXHIBITIONS
1982: Walker Art Center, Minneapolis, Minnesota ◦ 1981: Clifford Gallery, Pittsburgh Center for the Arts ◦ 1980: *William Wegman: Selected Works 1970-1979*, University of Colorado Museum, Boulder ◦ 1979: Holly Solomon Gallery, New York ◦ 1979: *William Wegman Retrospective*, Fine Arts Gallery, University of Wisconsin, Milwaukee ◦ 1977: Galerie Sonnabend, Paris ◦ 1973: Los Angeles County Museum of Art, Los Angeles.

SELECTED GROUP EXHIBITIONS
1981-1982: *Not Just for Laughs: The Art of Subversion*, The New Museum, New York ◦ 1981: *Biennial Exhibition*, Whitney Museum of American Art, New York ◦ 1980: *Ils se disent peintres, ils se disent photographes*, Musee d'Art Moderne de la Ville de Paris, Paris ◦ 1978: *Robert Cumming–William Wegman*, Baxter Art Gallery, California Institute of Technology, Pasadena, California ◦ 1975: *The Extended Document*, International Museum of Photography, George Eastman House, Rochester, New York ◦ 1971: *Project & Pier 18*, Museum of Modern Art, New York.

SELECTED MUSEUM AND PUBLIC COLLECTIONS
Art Gallery of Ontario, Toronto ◦ University Gallery, University of Massachusetts at Amherst ◦ Allen Memorial Art Museum, Oberlin College, Oberlin, Ohio ◦ The Museum of Fine Arts, Houston.